E. H. Lyon

Royal Education Commission

1886-8 - a summary of the final report, containing the conclusions and

recommendations of the Commissioners

E. H. Lyon

Royal Education Commission
1886-8 - a summary of the final report, containing the conclusions and recommendations of the Commissioners

ISBN/EAN: 9783337882198

Printed in Europe, USA, Canada, Australia, Japan

Cover: Foto ©Andreas Hilbeck / pixelio.de

More available books at **www.hansebooks.com**

ROYAL EDUCATION COMMISSION

1886-8.

A SUMMARY

OF THE

FINAL RE█████T

CONTAINING

THE CONCLUSIONS AND RECOM██████

OF

THE COMMISSIO█

BY

E. HERBERT LYON,

Assistant-Secretary to the Royal Com█████

London :

NATIONAL SOCIETY'S DEPOSITORY,

BROAD SANCTUARY, WESTMINSTER.

1888.

PREFACE.

THE great interest and anxiety with which the Final
Report of the Royal Education Commission has been
looked for by all classes in any way affected by the working
of the Elementary Education Acts, has induced me to
draw up a short summary of the conclusions arrived at,
and the recommendations made by the Commission in the
voluminous Report recently presented to Her Majesty.
In dealing with the Report I have had to bear in mind
that the space at my command would allow of nothing
more than a brief epitome of an important document. I
have, therefore, seldom reproduced the arguments upon
which the Commissioners have based the results of their
inquiry, save where they seemed to be of exceptional
importance. The same method has been followed in treat-
ing the testimony of individual witnesses.

A Report has been presented signed by fifteen
members of the Commission, consisting of the Chairman
(Viscount Cross), Cardinal Manning, the Duke of Norfolk,
the Earl of Harrowby, the Earl Beauchamp, the Bishop of
London, Lord Norton, Sir Francis Sandford, Archdeacon
B. F. Smith, the Rev. Dr. J. H. Rigg, Canon Gregory.
the Rev. Dr. T. D. C. Morse, Mr. C. H. Alderson, Mr. J. G.
Talbot, M.P., and Mr. Samuel Rathbone.

Another Report has been drawn up, signed in part by
Sir John Lubbock, M.P., Sir Bernhard Samuelson, M.P.,
and Mr. Sydney C. Buxton, M.P., and fully by the

following Commissioners: the Hon. E. Lyulph Stanley,
Dr. R. W. Dale, Mr. T. E. Heller, Mr. Henry Richard, M.P.,
and Mr. G. Shipton.

It has been somewhat difficult to deal intelligibly with
the Report of the "Minority," and to show clearly not
only how far they differed from the "Majority," but also
how far they were unanimous amongst themselves in
regard to the points under discussion.

The chapters in this volume have been summarised
in the same order and under the same headings as they
appear in the Report, and (where necessary) such
reservations as were made by any of the Commissioners
instead of being appended to the text, are for the sake of
greater clearness introduced as footnotes on the pages to
which they refer.

It has not been considered necessary in abridging the
Report of the "Minority" to go into such detail as in the
case of that of the "Majority"; their recommendations
however, are given, generally, in their own words.

                                  E. HERBERT LYON.

August, 1888.

MEMBERS OF THE COMMISSION.

THE VISCOUNT CROSS	*Secretary of State for India ; late Home Secretary.*
CARDINAL MANNING	*Roman Catholic Archbishop of Westminster.*
THE DUKE OF NORFOLK	*President of the Catholic Union of Great Britain.*
THE EARL OF HARROWBY	*Late Vice-President of the Council ; subsequently President of the Board of Trade.*
THE EARL BEAUCHAMP	*Member of H.M. Privy Council, and late Paymaster-General.*
THE LORD BISHOP OF LONDON	*Formerly Principal of Kneller Hall Training College ; Head Master of Rugby ; Member of the Schools Inquiry Commission of 1868-9.*
THE LORD NORTON	*Late Vice-President of the Council, and subsequently President of the Board of Trade.*
THE RIGHT HON. SIR FRANCIS SANDFORD, K.C.B.	*Late Permanent Secretary of the Education Department.*
THE HON. E. LYULPH STANLEY	*Late Member of the London School Board.*
SIR JOHN LUBBOCK, BART.	*M.P. for London University.*
SIR BERNHARD SAMUELSON, BART., M.P.	*Late Chairman of the Technical Instruction Commission.*
REV. J. H. RIGG, D.D.	*Principal of the Wesleyan Training College at Westminster ; late Member of the London School Board.*
R. W. DALE, ESQ., LL.D.	*Late Vice-Chairman of the Birmingham School Board ; Chairman of the Congregational Union of England and Wales, 1868-9.*
REV. ROBERT GREGORY	*Canon of St. Paul's ; Treasurer of the National Society ; late Member of the London School Board.*
THE VENERABLE B. F. SMITH	*Canon of Canterbury and Archdeacon of Maidstone.*

REV. T. D. COX MORSE, LL.D.	*Vicar of Christ Church, Newgate Street, and late Member of the London School Board.*
C. H. ALDERSON, ESQ.	*Charity Commissioner ; late one of H.M. Chief Inspectors of Schools.*
J. G. TALBOT, ESQ.	*M.P. for Oxford University ; late Secretary of the Board of Trade.*
SYDNEY C. BUXTON, ESQ., M.P.	*Late Member of the London School Board.*
THOMAS E. HELLER, ESQ.	*Secretary of the National Union of Elementary Teachers and Member of the London School Board.*
SAMUEL RATHBONE, ESQ.	*Chairman of the Liverpool School Board.*
HENRY RICHARD, ESQ.	*M.P. for Merthyr Tydvil.*
GEORGE SHIPTON, ESQ.	*Secretary of the London Trades Council.*

F. CAVENDISH BENTINCK, ESQ., *Secretary.*

E. HERBERT LYON, ESQ., *Assistant-Secretary.*

TABLE OF CONTENTS.

REPORT OF THE COMMISSION.

REPORT OF THE "MINORITY."

REPORT OF THE COMMISSION.

CHAPTER I.

SCHOOL SUPPLY.

THE Education Commission in making their final Report *Supply generally sufficient.* to Her Majesty have followed the order of the Syllabus of Subjects which has guided their inquiry, and which has been printed in each previous volume of their Report. The first head of their inquiry relates to the present supply of schools and the effectiveness of the Education Act of 1870* in providing for future requirements.

Mr. Cumin in his evidence stated that the supply is generally sufficient except in places where there is a continual increase in population, indeed that in every county *Excess in counties accounted for.* in England, excepting the London district, the supply is in excess of the requirements. This excess is attributed by him (i) to the number of large buildings originally built for Sunday schools now only partially occupied by the day schools held in them, (ii) to the greater attention now paid to the organization of infants' and babies' departments, and (iii) to the multiplication of class rooms for separate teaching.

* Sec. V, Act 1870 :—"There shall be provided for every school district a sufficient amount of accommodation in public elementary schools available for all the children resident in such district for whose elementary education efficient and suitable provision is not otherwise made."

B

The decrease of population in many rural and mining districts is a further reason alleged for local excess in school supply.

For what proportion of the population provision is to be made. Reference is made to the Report of the Education Department, 1886-7, in which one-sixth of the entire population is assumed to be the basis upon which provision should be made, in accordance with the instructions issued to Inspectors of Returns in 1871, and the Commission say that under present conditions they are disposed to agree with the basis upon which this calculation is made. That in certain localities accommodation has been provided in excess of this estimate they attribute to the increased attractiveness of the schools, which induces a larger number of children of a better class to attend, and also to the provision of the Act of 1876 which compels backward children to remain at school up to the age of 14.

Provision for infants. Mr. Cumin stated that the Department has no uniform rule for the provision of accommodation for children between the ages of three and five, and that though children between those ages are generally considered capable of going to school and earning a grant, yet this does not imply that accommodation is to be supplied in every case.

Deficiency of school accommodation for infants in London. The question having arisen as to whether in London a deficiency of accommodation for infants exists, the Commission are of opinion that it is not so serious as at first sight might appear, and in support of this they cite the Census returns for 1881, which show the proportion of children of school age in London to the total population to be considerably below that of the country at large.

By whom are the require- The Department are kept informed, Mr. Cumin said, of the requirements of each district by the Inspectors, who are bound to report upon the existence of any deficiency; that while School Boards in their own districts are the primary judges as to the sufficiency or deficiency of accommodation, and School Attendance Committees in non-school board districts, the Department is ultimately responsible for deciding whether further provision is necessary. *ments ascertained.*

On the vexed question as to whether a School Board has a prior right in its own district to supply a deficiency of accommodation, the Commission say that the existence of such a right is asserted by the Department, and grounded upon the 18th Section of the Act of 1870;* as a consequence offers on the part of voluntary bodies to supply an actual deficiency have in many cases been refused by the Department, so that the schools if they had been built would have been excluded from a grant. Mr. Cumin explained that the action of the Department in giving the prior right to a School Board has been based on their interpretation of the Act of 1870, namely, "that as the School Board are bound by the 10th Section of the Act of 1870,† to supply the deficiency, so under the 18th Section they are afterwards entitled, if they insist on doing so, to supply whatever deficiency may from time to time arise." *Prior right to supply accommodation.*

Whether School Boards can divest themselves of this prior right, the Commission say that, although Mr. Cumin appears to assume the existence of such a power, in *Can Boards give up their prior right.*

---

* Sec. XVIII, Act 1870 :—"The School Board shall maintain and keep efficient every school provided by such Board, and shall from time to time provide such additional school accommodation as is, in their opinion, necessary in order to supply a sufficient amount of public school accommodation for their district."

† By this section the time is reduced within which it is allowable to supply a deficiency in any district, before a School Board is compulsorily formed, from 12 to 6 months; and makes the election of a School Board, when a deficiency is not supplied, imperative.

practice there have been important exceptions, notably in **Willesden case.** the Willesden case, in which the Department compelled the School Board to supply a deficiency which formed the ground for its establishment, under pain of being declared in default if it allowed a clergyman to step into its place and supply the deficiency.

Grievances. This official interpretation of the law as to the right of supply, the Commission say, has been the cause of much controversy and complaint, especially in the case of the Roman Catholic body. Dissatisfaction is felt first at the action of the Department in allowing School Boards practically to decide whether a proposed voluntary school is necessary or not, and further in refusing to exercise the discretionary power conferred upon them by the 98th Section of the Act of 1870,* viz.: to give or withhold grants to unnecessary schools,—School Boards, it is alleged, being more liable than the Department to have a hostile feeling towards the promoters.

In dealing with this subject the Commission express the opinion that some check ought to be placed on the multiplication of schools claiming to be supported out of the education grant, and that that check can hardly be placed in other hands than those of the Education Department, to which it has been committed by statute, and should not be placed in the hands of any local body.

Dan-y-craig case. In illustration of the practice of the Department to remit to a School Board the question whether a new school is unnecessary, reference is made to the well-known Dan-y-craig case, in which a Roman Catholic school in course of erection was pronounced to be unnecessary by the Department, owing to the Swansea

---

* This section subjects Board Schools to the same rule as voluntary schools in respect to the refusal of aid if they are unnecessary.

School Board refusing to withdraw their objection to its being admitted to an annual grant and claiming to exercise their prior right to supply the existing deficiency. After reviewing Mr. Cumin's evidence on this case, the Commission express their opinion that the interpretation put upon Section 98 of the Act of 1870 seems somewhat strained. They think that the Department was in error in leaving in the hands of the School Board a decision which the law had committed to them, viz., whether the school in question was unnecessary; and afterwards in failing to exercise their own discretion to give or withhold a grant to an unnecessary school.

The Commission are of opinion that the remedy for these grievances lies in a more liberal interpretation of the word "suitability," and in a close adherence to the spirit of the provisions of the Act of 1870, but that to abolish all restrictions on grants to unnecessary schools would prove injurious to the interests of the very schools which it is sought to uphold. **Remedy for grievances.**

With regard to the definition of the word "suitability" as applied to schools in the Act of 1870, the Commission restrict themselves to recording Mr. Cumin's view of Section V of that Act. They say:— **"Suitability."**

" According to this (Mr. Cumin's) interpretation, the Act of
" 1870 provides, that in any school district, if there be not
"already efficient and sufficient accommodation, which is
" also ' suitable,' or ' such as the parents could not reasonably
" object to on religious grounds,' then the law shall step in
"and see that a public elementary school is established,
" in which the question of ' suitability' will not arise,
" because the school is *ipso facto* suitable."

The working of the provisions of the 23rd section of the **Transfer of**

schools to School Boards. Act of 1870* is alleged to inflict an injury on undenominational schools. It is said first that thereby the influence of trustees and founders is set aside, the fate of the school being left in the hands of an uncertain and changing body, often composed of those who may have previously taken no active interest in the school, and secondly that the terms of an agreement with the School Board have often been sanctioned by the Education Department which have unduly interfered with the original trusts.

The Commission, in view of the friction thus created, recommend for the proper transfer of a school held under trust : 1. That the consent of a majority of the trustees should be necessary. 2. That beyond the requirements of the Education Acts the Department should not sanction any agreement at variance with the original trust; and 3. That no structural expenses, involving a loan, should be incurred, without the consent of the trustees who lease the building.

Supply of future deficiency. Having considered the whole question of providing against future deficiency of accommodation, the Commission think that a general inquiry into the school supply of the country at large, similar to that commenced in 1871, ought to be held periodically—say every five years—and that in the interval between any two such inquiries, voluntary schools (whether provided to meet a numerical deficiency or specially required by any part of the population) ought to be recognized by the Department as entitled to claim annual grants, on the same terms as board schools.

Who may use the supply. As to the class of children to whom school accommodation is open under the Act of 1870, the Commission are of opinion that although Mr. Forster's Act has given the

* Section XXIII, Act 1870, prescribes in detail the conditions under which a school may be transferred by the managers to a school board.

legal right to all parents, including those well able to provide education for their children, to send them to a State-aided or rate-supported school (a result which was not perhaps fully considered during the passing of the Act), the use of such schools by the latter class of persons would in practice not be likely to extend itself if a proper system of secondary education were organized throughout the country, open by means of exhibitions to children from elementary schools.

CHAPTER II.

STRUCTURAL SUITABILITY OF THE PRESENT SCHOOL SUPPLY.

THE proportion of the population for which the Commission remark they have shown that school provision is needed, namely, one-sixth of the population, and in certain districts one-fifth, is said to have been adequately provided for, although it is pointed out in the Report that the suitability of the actual space provided must obviously affect that conclusion.

Quality of school accommodation.

The Commission report that great difference exists in the suitability of school premises, since no uniform standard has been insisted upon, but that the estimate of what is required in the way of buildings and appliances is now higher than it used to be, owing to the improvement carried out under the direction of H.M. Inspectors. With regard to the difference in the minimum area of accommodation insisted on by the Department between that provided by voluntary effort and that created by School

Boards out of loans, namely, in the one case 8 square feet, and in the other 10 square feet per child, the latter in the view of the Commission more nearly represents the demands that have to be met; and now that the great strain entailed by the Act of 1870 in supplying accommodation has passed, they think the State should be more exacting in requiring for all children a proper amount of air and space, suitable premises, airiness and lightness of site, and reasonable extent of playground.

The further opinion is expressed that the proper measure of a school's accommodation should be the seat room provided rather than the simple calculation of superficial area.

Whilst recognizing it as a hardship that any sudden demand for more ample accommodation should be made on schools built before 1870, the Commission consider it a most important rule of the Department that 10 square feet should be the minimum accommodation for each child in average attendance in all future buildings.

These observations, it is added, apply in some degree to the cubical contents of schoolrooms, which the Department require in all new schools to be on a minimum scale of 100 cubic feet for each child in average attendance.

The Commission come to the conclusion that, in order to bring existing schools up to the higher estimate of accommodation, a liberal allowance of time should be given to managers for making alterations, so as to avoid any undue burden which many districts might otherwise feel; it is also thought that the pressure of H.M. Inspectors on the managers will be exerted more advantageously than any hard-and-fast rule of the Department.*

* Sir Francis Sandford does not think that this requirement should be enforced in the case of schools erected by the aid of a grant, according to plans recommended and insisted on by the Department, and providing 8 feet per scholar, since some of the best and most popular voluntary schools would be the first to suffer.

Attention is drawn to the fact that, in recommending 10 square feet as the provision for each child, such accommodation is needed for the number in average attendance, and not for those whose names are on the books.

As to the school fittings, it is not thought advisable to lay down any absolute rule, except that the primary consideration in the equipment of a school should be its suitability to the age, size, and physical comfort of the children. **School fittings.**

The value of playgrounds is specially dwelt upon, as having an undoubted influence in giving children a liking for school, and in affording special opportunities for moral training when they are released from discipline; and the Commission think that the Department as a rule should recommend the provision of a playground, and if possible separate ones for the two sexes, in the erection of all new schools over which they have any control. **Playgrounds.**

CHAPTER III.

SCHOOL MANAGEMENT.

In defining school management the Commission point out that as schools exist both for the purpose of forming the character as well as of cultivating the intelligence of children, the duties of school managers will accordingly be divided into two branches, viz.:— **Management defined.**

1. Such duties as can be conducted by managers at a distance from the school.

2. Those duties for the performance of which direct contact with the school and personal intercourse with the teachers and scholars are necessary.

**Qualifica-
tions for
each
branch.**

In reviewing the evidence given before the Commission, the Report goes on to say that the duties of these two branches of management in most cases may easily be combined, except where a great many schools are carried on under the control of one board, as is the case in London.

For the work of school management in committee, there are required breadth of view, business habits, administrative ability, and the power of working harmoniously with others; whilst personal oversight of schools demands more especially, interest in school work, sympathy with teachers and scholars, together with residence in proximity to the school, and leisure time during school hours.

**Manage-
ment of
voluntary
schools.**

In dealing with the question of the management of voluntary schools, the Commission make the following statement:—

" For the management of those voluntary schools which have
" been built with aid from the Government Grant, the
" Education Department in very early days made definite
" provision, by inserting in the Trust Deed of each school a
" certain Management Clause differing in some respects
" according to the description of the school. These specified
" the qualifications, and subsequent method of election of
" the managing body, the original body of managers having
" been nominated by the promoters of the school. To a
" body so constituted the whole direction of the school was
" committed by the clauses which were imposed by the
" Government as a condition of a building grant and accepted
" by the founders of the schools; while in the case of
" Church of England schools the superintendence of the
" religious and moral instruction was assigned to the clergy-
" man of the parish. A similar arrangement prevailed in the
" case of Roman Catholic schools. The returns made by
" the managers of voluntary schools throughout specimen

" districts of England . . . . show that such bodies
" of managers are almost universally in existence, whatever
" be their degree of vitality, and that they comprise persons
" in very various social positions. Nor do they exist merely
" on paper. The returns made annually to the Department
" from every school receiving a grant require the signature
" of three persons to authenticate the numerous particulars
" required to be certified; though of these three persons only
" one need be a manager."

The Commission emphatically condemn the "farming" **" Farmed " schools.**
of schools by teachers, in evasion of the rule forbidding a
school to be carried on for private profit, and say that
effective measures ought to be taken to render the
continuance of such a system impossible. Although it is
recognized that in some places the management must
inevitably fall into the hands of one individual, the
Commission think that voluntary schools, where it
is practicable, should be under efficient and active
boards of managers.

With regard to the accounts of voluntary schools, the **Scrutiny of Accounts.**
Commission recommend that they shall be as open to
public inspection as those of board schools.

So far as personal and sympathetic supervision is **Merits of voluntary management.**
concerned, the Report says that much of the evidence is
favourable to the voluntary system of management, and
in support of this conclusion the evidence of the following
witnesses is quoted, viz.: Mr. Sharpe, Archdeacon Norris,
Mr. Stewart, Canon Warburton, and the Chairman of the
School Attendance Committee of the Leek Union.

The Commission do not think that representatives **Who should manage voluntary schools.**
of the ratepayers should be introduced on the managing
boards of voluntary schools, as suggested by several
witnesses; so long as these schools receive no aid from the

rates, they see no sufficient reason why, in this respect, their trust deeds should be set aside; they recommend, however, that, where it is possible, representatives of the parents of the scholars shall be introduced into the managing body, though they should not form a preponderating element.

School Board management.

School Board management is next dealt with, and reference is made to a passage of Mr. Diggle's evidence, where he describes at some length the system of dual management now adopted by the London School Board, local managers being entrusted with large responsibilities under the supervision of the School Management Committee.

Local managers.

A description is given in the Report of the methods of school management adopted by the School Boards of Liverpool and Birmingham, which shows that while in the former place the School Board gradually entrust the entire management of each school to a local board of managers, carefully initiated at first into their duties, the schools under the Birmingham School Board have no voluntary managers, but a staff of local inspectors employed to visit and report upon them.

On this point the Commission express an opinion that although local managers are sometimes dispensed with, it would be very advantageous for the School Board (and especially the larger Boards) always to associate with themselves local managers in the supervision of their schools, while managers of board schools might be relieved of some of that routine work which at present tends to limit the general supervision they can exercise over schools; but the employment of local inspectors, it is thought, can only lead to their imperfectly discharging their functions as managers.

In comparing the two systems of board and voluntary management, the Commission say :—

General comparison between board and voluntary management.

"If it were needful to strike a balance between the efficiency
"of the two systems of board and voluntary school
"management, the evidence before us would lead us to
"divide the honours. If it be asked under which system
"of management that branch of administration which can
"be transacted outside the school is most vigorously con-
"ducted, it would be impossible to deny the superiority of
"the management of the School Board dispensing the
"money of the ratepayers. If, however, we look for the
"closest supervision of the school and the most effective
"sympathy between managers and teachers, or between
"managers and scholars, we should feel, on the whole,
"bound to pronounce in favour of the efficiency of voluntary
"management. It is in the combination of the advantages
"of both systems that we look for progress in the future."

Special attention is drawn to the co-operation which
has been successfully attempted in Liverpool between board
and voluntary managers by means of a conference formed
for the purpose of arriving at a uniform system of management. The Commission think the extension of such a
system would further be beneficial in mitigating unwhole-
some rivalry between the two systems, and that voluntary
and board school managers have much to learn from each
other.

Liverpool conference of managers.

In recommending, in conclusion, a system of co-operation amongst managers of voluntary schools, as practised
in the diocese of Rochester, and in Huddersfield and
Bradford, where inspectors are now employed by voluntary associations to visit Church schools, the Commission
express a strong opinion that for isolated schools this form
of voluntary combination is likely to strengthen their
position not only financially but also educationally, and

Co-opera-tion of voluntary schools.

that some similar combination for the purposes of instruction by experts in such subjects as cookery and the rudiments of elementary science, might be extended to voluntary schools under schemes similar to those carried out by the Northern School of Cookery and by the Birmingham School Board.

CHAPTER IV.

HER MAJESTY'S INSPECTORS OF SCHOOLS.

Staff. THE staff of Inspectors is reported to consist of the following :—

    12 Chief Inspectors

    120 Inspectors

    30 Sub-Inspectors

    152 Inspectors' Assistants,

the work of the Education Department being carried on by 21 Examiners under the supervision of the Secretaries.

An Inspector at the Department. The suggestion to place one of H.M. Inspectors in the Department as an Assistant Secretary to advise on matters connected with inspection, meets with no approval, though the Commission are not opposed to a vacancy in the Secretariat being filled by the appointment of an inspector.

Qualifications. With regard to the high intellectual qualifications which have hitherto been exacted for the appointment to the post both of Examiner and Inspector, namely, a University degree and a first or second class in honours, the Commission are of opinion that although these requirements may have hitherto possibly checked unsuitable appointments, yet that some modifications in the present rules are desirable.

First as to the admission of teachers to the in- *Admission of teachers to the inspectorate.* spectorate. The evidence given by teachers themselves on the point is said to have been by no means unanimous, some strongly objecting to have their schools inspected by those who had been members of the teaching body. Of those not professionally interested in the matter, Mr. Matthew Arnold, Mr. Diggle, and Mr. Fitch declared themselves favourable to the proposal to recruit the body of inspectors from the ranks of elementary teachers, while Mr. Oakeley and Mr. Sharpe took the opposite view. The Commission, after considering the evidence given on *Conclusion.* both sides, come to the conclusion that while the public service requires inspectors to be men of wide and liberal training, yet there are some of the elementary teachers who possess the high qualifications required in a competent inspector, and that it is neither fair nor wise by artificial barriers to prevent them from rising to the rank of inspector. They further consider that such an opening would tend to elevate the tone and character of their important profession.

The next point dealt with is the examination of *Examination by specialists.* schools where special subjects are taught. The Commission think it important that the inspector should have a thorough knowledge of such subjects, since an intelligent and efficient examination will effectually tend to remedy mechanical and superficial instruction. This, it is remarked, was urged by several witnesses as being especially necessary in science examinations, which must be partially oral, and the Commission recommend that *Conclusion.* although a knowledge of science cannot reasonably be demanded of all the ordinary inspectors, yet in future it

would be desirable, in regard to a larger proportion of them
than at present, that special weight should be given to a
knowledge of this subject in the appointment to the
inspectorate; at the same time they think that when
specialists examine they ought also to have had some experience of the conditions of elementary school education.

Female Inspectors. The further question having arisen as to the employment of female inspectors in visiting infant schools, and
examining the lower standards, the Commission, after
stating that there are serious practical difficulties in the
way of their general employment, make the following
suggestion :—

> " We think, however, that the experiment might be tried in
> " large towns of appointing a sub-inspectress to assist the
> " head inspectors in the examination of infant schools and
> " of the earlier standards in other schools. They should
> " themselves have been teachers in elementary schools, or
> " should have had experience as governesses in one or other
> " of the training colleges. We have been much struck by
> " the ability, earnestness, and good sense of several of the
> " mistresses who have come before us to give evidence."

Inspectors' assistants. Complaints were made that the initial salary of inspectors' assistants is insufficient, and that in consequence the
best men are deterred from applying for the post. The
Commission are of opinion that these assistants should be
chosen from the pick of the elementary schoolmasters
who have acquired adequate experience, and accordingly
recommend that the initial salary should be raised to £200
a year.

**More fre-
quent
change of
Inspectors.** It was suggested, the Report says, to mitigate what is
called the autocracy of an inspector in his own district,
either by enlarging the area and placing it under a joint
board of inspectors, or by a more frequent change of

district. The Commission however think the former scheme impracticable, and that the latter would be of no advantage, since not only is long connection with a district valuable in bringing about a good understanding between inspectors and managers, but also frequent change would produce uncertainty in the examinations, besides being very costly to the country and the inspectors.

Passing on to consider how a uniform standard of examination amongst such a large body of inspectors may best be attained, the Commission report that from the official evidence they have received, great pains appear already to be taken to establish uniformity of judgment among the district inspectors by conference and comparison of results in each division, and also by a careful examination on the part of the Department of the tabulated results of inspections, any wide discrepancies between one district and another being brought to the notice of the chief inspectors. Although the Commission think that approximation to a common standard of judgment has been reached, and that further progress is likely to be made, they suggest as likely to still further produce uniformity of standard, that chief inspectors should cease to have charge of small districts of their own, so that their whole time may be given up to supervising the larger areas, and to reviewing the work of the inspectors in their division when complaints are made to the Department. For the suggestion made in some quarters that a more lenient test is applied to the examination of voluntary schools than of board schools, the Commission say they have no reason to believe there is any ground whatever. *Uniform standard of examination.*

The same tests applied to all classes of schools.

With regard to visits without notice, commonly called " surprise visits," brief reference to the evidence given by *Visits without notice.*

C

several inspectors on the subject seems on the whole to show that such visits may be of considerable advantage; and the Commission, in order to admit of more frequent visits without notice than are at present possible, and also that more time may be given to the annual examinations of schools and pupil-teachers, are of opinion that some re-arrangement of the work, or an increase in the strength of the inspecting staff, is necessary.

" More frequent occasional visits," the Report goes on to say, "are not suggested as a means of detecting abuses, but " rather to enable the inspector by the observation of a " school under its normal conditions to acquaint himself with " the general tone of the school and with the method of " instruction, and to offer friendly advice to the teachers on " any points on which they may stand in need."

Publication of reports. Mention is made of the fact that formerly the Education Department published the Inspectors' Reports of Schools in the Blue Books, but that owing to the expense which would now be involved in printing the Reports of some 25,000 different schools, the practice could not be resumed. The Commission however are of opinion that the annual reports of voluntary schools might with advantage be made as public as those of board schools.

Complaints against inspectors, as to method of examination. Numerous complaints, it is stated, have been made by teachers as to the method of conducting examinations, and although the Commission remark that, in making many of these complaints, the requirements of the Code have probably been lost sight of, they at the same time call the attention of inspectors to the great difference between a competitive and a non-competitive examination; that as the aim of the latter should be to find out what the children know and not what they do not know, it is a mistake to put questions which are too hard. For the further complaint that in the examination in dictation **As to dictation.** children are confused by the inspector's voice, to which they are unaccustomed, and so mistake his words, the Commission think there is some foundation, and recommend that the passage selected by the inspector should in future be read out by the teacher.

To meet the alleged grievance that complaints of **Attention paid to complaints.** injustice are withheld from the notice of the Department from fear of offending the inspector, and lest a reduction of the grant might follow, the Commission think it should be made clear that the Department are willing and anxious to examine all such complaints, and that a school will not suffer in consequence.

Although mention was made in evidence of the alleged **Conclusion.** infringement by inspectors of their instructions, of which, however, it is said no direct evidence was forthcoming, and further of the undue protraction of examinations, which in some districts is attributable to an insufficient staff of inspectors, the Commission express their opinion that in the matter of inspection, though the present system may be susceptible of improvements in the directions indicated, the country has been on the whole well served, especially since the establishment of a graded system of inspection.

CHAPTER V.

TEACHERS AND STAFF.

UNDER this head the Report draws attention to the import- **Sufficiency of present supply.** ance attached in the earliest days of the administration of the parliamentary grant to securing an adequate supply of good teachers, as shown both in the aid granted to training colleges, and by augmentations made to the salaries of teachers proportionate to the class of their certificates. After giving statistics to show the increase of the teaching staff between the years 1869 and 1886, the Commission proceed to estimate the sufficiency of the present supply. They say that the evidence seems to prove that whilst the number of trained male teachers is somewhat in excess of the present demand, there is still a growing demand for fully qualified female teachers.

Efficiency of present supply. As to the quality of this supply, the Commission pay the following tribute to the professional zeal and integrity of the staff of teachers : " We are glad to state our opinion, that, as a whole, the present body of teachers are a very honourable body, and have a great sense of their duties to the children in regard to the formation of their character, and their moral guidance." It is said that teachers themselves acknowledge that there is less educational enthusiasm than formerly, and that less time is now devoted by teachers' associations to educational questions, which is attributed by them to the unfavourable conditions under which they now work.

Female teachers. The employment of females of superior social position and general culture as teachers, the Report says, has been tried with much success in Roman Catholic schools, their labours producing very refining and excellent results. Attention is drawn to the special regulations of the Code of 1882 to induce university graduates and women over 18 who have passed recognized university examinations to enter the teaching profession, by admitting them to become assistant teachers after passing the admission examination to training colleges, though in no case, it appears, have these provisions been taken advantage of.

Complaints were made by the teachers as to the large **Untrained teachers.** number of untrained certificated teachers, who are said to often prove unsatisfactory, and to stand in the way of those who are well-qualified finding employment. A table is given showing the numbers of trained and untrained certificated teachers, there being in all 23,180 of the former to 18,737 of the latter. Suggestions were received for reducing the number of untrained certificated teachers by diminishing the facilities for obtaining a certificate without training. The Commission however think that, in making any such change, it should be remembered that there are some untrained teachers with a natural aptitude for teaching who could not be excluded from the profession without real loss to schools.

In dealing with the question of teachers' salaries, men- **Salaries.** tion is made of the great rise which has taken place during the last 30 years, and the Commission are glad to learn from the evidence of several witnesses and from their own statistical inquiries, that the system of fluctuating salaries is giving way before that of fixed salaries in voluntary as well as in board schools, and they are of opinion that the teachers' salaries should be fixed, and in no degree dependent upon the grant.

As to the endorsement of certificates, the opinions of **Endorsement of certificates.** some of H.M. Inspectors, differing a good deal among themselves, are simply cited, without an opinion being given on the part of the Commission.

The question of teachers' pensions is said to be some- **Pensions.** what complicated by past treatment. Lord Lingen gave it as his opinion that the authors of the Minutes of 1846 under which the first offer of pensions was made, did not contemplate the introduction of a general system of pensions, but only an aid to schools in removing inefficient teachers. Subsequently, the Report says, the Code of 1876 specified the teachers entitled to apply for pensions to be those employed on May 9th, 1862, when the original Minute was cancelled, and it has consequently been contended that those who were induced to become pupil-teachers and were at the training colleges at that date on the strength of the old Pension Minute, are entitled to its benefits; a contention upon which no opinion is expressed. The Commission, after considering the evidence given both by inspectors and teachers, and also the answers to their statistical inquiries with regard to the establishment of a system of pensions, say that there is now a very general consensus of opinion in its favour. The Commission would be glad to see some superannuation scheme introduced, though they think that the compulsion upon existing teachers to contribute to its fund should be indirect rather than direct, and should be enforced by the action of the managers rather than as a legal obligation upon the

Scheme proposed. teachers. Accordingly it is recommended that the facilities offered by the Post Office for the purchase of deferred annuities should be taken advantage of, and that managers should see that in future every teacher is possessed of a deferred annuity of £30 in the case of men, and £20 in that of women, to come into operation at the age of 55. It is also suggested that, in the case of those so assured as well as of teachers already assured in other offices, the Department should supplement the annuity of a retiring teacher—also through the Post Office—by a maximum augmentation of not more than £15, according to length of service; and that the scheme should be made compulsory on all teachers certificated after a certain date to be fixed by Parliament; the funds for this augmentation being provided by a deduction of £1 per cent. from the annual grants to elementary schools.

As to the staff necessary for the proper working of a **staff.**
school, the Commission regard the evidence both of
inspectors and teachers as establishing the insufficiency of
the present Code requirements, calling attention to the
Education Department Report of 1886-7, which shows
that the total staff of the country exceeded the Code **Code**
minimum by 49 per cent., and they recommend that the **minimum.**
minimum should be considerably raised, a change which,
it is shown, would only affect the schools that are so
understaffed as to need the application of pressure on
them.

Considerable difference of opinion was found to exist **Should**
among the witnesses as to whether the head teacher **head teachers**
should be reckoned on the minimum staff; and the Com- **count on**
mission think that whilst it would be undesirable for a **the staff?**
head master not to give general superintendence to the
whole work of the school, at the same time it would be a
matter for regret if he were to dissociate himself from the
actual teaching. Further it is thought that if the general
requirements of the Code as to staff be raised, it might well
be left to managers and head teachers to organize their
schools as they please, subject to the inspector's report
that the results of the teaching are satisfactory.

Great importance is attached by the Commission to **size of**
keeping classes within a reasonable size. In the **classes.**
evidence given to them it is suggested that the average
maximum should be 40 for an ordinary class and 25 for
the highest.

With regard to the pupil-teacher system several wit- **pupil-**
nesses are quoted whose opinions on the subject are much **teachers.**
at variance : some severely criticising it, whilst others, -
including two Principals of Training Colleges, speak
strongly in its favour. The Commission, however, can

recommend no other adequate source from which teachers may be supplied, and think that the system should be upheld, subject to the improvement taking place in the educational training of the pupil-teachers, which is at **Difficulty of finding pupil-teachers.** present defective. The difficulty of finding a sufficient supply of suitable pupil-teachers will be met, it is thought, by recurring to the former practice of allowing them to be engaged at the age of 13 for five years.

Centre system. Regarding the working of the system of instructing pupil-teachers at centres, reference is made to the evidence borne by Mr. MacCarthy to its success as carried out by the Birmingham School Board; to that of Mr. Hance, speaking of the favourable experience of the Liverpool School Board; and to the approval of the plan adopted by the London School Board, as expressed by Mr. Diggle, its chairman ; as well as to the satisfactory results, as shown by a tabulated record, of the examination for Queen's scholarships of the pupil-teachers so instructed.

Complaints against pupil-teachers. Many and various complaints against the pupil-teacher system itself are noted in the Report, together with proposals for its improvement. Special reference is made to the Inspectors' Reports of Training Colleges, as to the imperfect preparation of in-coming students. The Commission think that the inspectors should pay more attention to the annual examination, and that it would be well to so re-arrange the conditions of apprenticeship as to give pupil-teachers, on reaching the age of 16, more facilities to withdraw from the profession if they dislike it, and to managers to enable them to get rid of those who are unsuitable.

Recommendations. The Report concludes with the following recommendations :—

1. That pupil-teachers should be allowed more time

during school hours for their own studies, and (subject to no interference with the responsibility of head teachers) that the instruction of pupil-teachers should be supplemented by central class teaching in the compulsory and additional subjects.

2. That extra Government grants for this purpose should be given to managers of voluntary schools and to School Boards.

3. That where the centre system is impossible, these extra grants should also be given if other special means of instruction are successfully employed.*

CHAPTER VI.

TRAINING COLLEGES.

On the subject of Training, the Report opens with some **Statistics.** statistics concerning the existing training colleges, which show the number, inclusive of those of all denominations, to have been 43 in 1886, the expenditure in the same year being £167,647, towards which the State contributed

---

* Sir Francis Sandford expresses his fear that the Commission have dealt with the pupil-teachers too much us pupils, and too little as teachers; since in giving them more time for private study, the teaching power of a school will be weakened, and the raising of the standard of examination will tend to over-pressure. He prefers the old system of instruction to the centre system, which he believes is attended with serious danger and disadvantages, and thinks that in large towns the instruction of pupil-teachers in each school might be divided amongst the certificated teachers under the supervision of the head-teachers.

£115,275, and the total number of male students 1,391, and of females 1,881.

Testimony of the inspectors as to results. The past and present inspectors of training colleges who were examined, namely, Mr. Sharpe, Canon Warburton, Mr. Oakeley, and Mr. Fitch, all bore testimony to the good results of the religious, moral, and intellectual influence of these institutions, though each qualified his **Criticisms.** expression of satisfaction by certain criticisms. Thus Mr. Sharpe would curtail the hours of study, Canon Warburton expresses his disappointment with the intellectual acquirements and technical skill obtained in the female colleges, and Mr. Oakeley and Mr. Fitch are not satisfied with the practising schools. Reference is also made to the evidence of other witnesses who spoke unfavourably of the present system, amongst them being Dr. Crosskey and Mr. MacCarthy, both of Birmingham; and to the testimony of Mr. Matthew Arnold, who expressed his preference for the German, French, and Swiss systems. The Commission however agree with Archdeacon Norris in thinking that the colleges "do wonders in the two years" with the raw material they have to handle, and further they are of opinion that until the candidates for admission are better prepared much substantial improvement cannot be looked for.

Complaints of restrictions on training. Many complaints, the Report says, have been directed against the existing system, because of the inaccessibility of the colleges to students of all religious denominations, and the insufficient number of undenominational colleges. One witness contended that the support of denominational colleges by the State is wrong in principle. With this view however the Commission do not agree, so long as the majority of schools and scholars are denominational, and the supply of trained teachers is good; they think also

that the contention comes too late after the State has
entered into binding engagements with these institutions.

As to the claims made for the introduction of a con- Conscience
science clause into training colleges, the Commission clause.
strongly hold that the compliance with such a demand
would have an injurious effect on the domestic and moral
discipline in denominational or undenominational colleges
by granting liberty of exemption from all religious
instruction, and from all common acts of worship in the
college. Great importance is attached to the opinions of
those inspectors whose experience in connection with
training colleges is of the widest, all of whom deprecate
the proposal, regarding as inadmissible such a fundamental change as the imposition of a conscience clause
would involve. The Commission say that their recommendations for giving enlarged facilities for training are
based on the supposition that the present arrangements of
the Department with the denominational training colleges
will not be seriously disturbed; at the same time they see
no reason why grants should not be made to any residential training college henceforth established by private
liberality on an undenominational basis, and with a conscience clause in the trust deed.

Objection is taken to a reduction of the maintenance Reduction
grant to training colleges by the State as suggested by of grant.
some witnesses, since it is thought that the State gets full
value for its annual expenditure, and that high entrance
fees would place an obstacle in the way of the admission to college of students of humble origin, so many
of whom in past years have become most efficient
teachers.

As to the proposal for an extension of training to a third Extension
year, advocated by the Principals of certain training of training

to third
year.

colleges, and by other witnesses, the Commission are of opinion that much may be said for it, that our masters require a more thorough training, and extended over a longer period, and they only hesitate to recommend an additional year of training from a doubt as to its feasibility at present; it is thought however that at convenient centres picked students from college might even now continue their instruction for a third year.

Serious objections are regarded as standing in the way of the suggestion that this third year should be spent at Oxford or Cambridge, among them being the additional expense that would thereby be involved.

Day
training
colleges.

The Commission are satisfied by the evidence that greater facilities are required for training. Amongst the schemes laid before them for this purpose are those for the establishment of day training colleges as submitted by Mr. MacCarthy, Vice-President of the Birmingham School Board, and by Mr. Cumin.

Mr. Mac
Carthy's
scheme.

By the former it is proposed to establish ten or twelve day colleges in large towns, each accommodating 250 students of both sexes, who would enter at the age of 16, and remain 5 years, a preparatory course of secondary instruction being also provided for them between the age of 14, the time when most children leave school, and 16, the entrance age to college. The total cost to the State is estimated at £60,200. This arrangement the Commission think is open to several objections, such as the supersession of the pupil-teacher system, and a claim by existing colleges for largely increased grants, to which these proposals would lead.

Mr. Cumin's
scheme.

By Mr. Cumin's scheme it is proposed to utilise as day training colleges existing educational institutions to which practising schools may be attached, a grant of £25 being paid by the State to every Queen's scholar trained at the day training college towards his maintenance, and in respect of each day scholar a further sum of £10 to the managing committee in aid of the cost of providing instruction. With Mr. Cumin's recommendation the Commission do not wholly agree, and they cite the evidence of several important witnesses who concur in the view that the system of day training colleges can never be as effective as that of residential colleges.

Passing on to consider the plan for affiliating training colleges to local university colleges, the details of such a scheme are given, as explained by Professor Bodington, for the training of teachers in connection with the Yorkshire College at Leeds. Arrangements it is said could be made to admit thirty or forty pupils at a cost of £55 each for maintenance as well as for instruction in the college subjects and professional subjects, the results being tested by both a Government and an University examination, the certificate obtained leading up to a degree in the University to which the local college is affiliated. *Affiliation of training colleges to local colleges.*

With regard to the schemes submitted to them, the Commission report as follows :— *Conclusion and recommendations.*

" Considering the demand that already exists for more ample or
" more generally available opportunities of training, and the
" importance of giving every facility for training to those
" who now obtain certificates without it ; considering,
" further, that such schemes as those submitted to us would,
" in their nature, be tentative, that they would not involve a
" large outlay of capital, and would only be adopted when
" local circumstances seemed to invite the adaptation of
" some existing educational machinery to this purpose, we
" think it might be well that some such experiment should
" be made, subject to the condition, that only a limited

" number of students should receive Government assistance
" towards their training. It would be obviously impossible
" to limit the number of those who were desirous of being
" trained in such colleges at their own expense. But such a
" number only of students should be paid for by the Depart-
" ment as are found practically necessary to complete the
" supply of trained teachers who should be largely sub-
" stituted for the present mass of untrained and uncer-
" tificated teachers."

Conditions to be fulfilled. The following points are mentioned as those which would have to be considered and met by Parliament in any fresh legislation required to give effect to their recommendations in favour of additional facilities for training:—

(1) The question of security for the religious and moral instruction; (2) the constitution of the governing body; (3) the re-adjustment of the financial relations of the governing body with the State; and (4) the regulation of the supply of day trained teachers in some fair proportion to the demand.

Day students in residential colleges. A suggestion by Mr. Cumin that existing training colleges should be permitted, though not compelled, to take day students, appears to the Commission to have very great recommendations, and they think that those students whose parents are of a different denomination from that of the college, might be received without being required to join in the family worship of the college, or receiving any religious instruction to which the parents object.

In considering the question of day training colleges, the Commission state their belief that while the uninterrupted influence of a boarding college is of the greatest advantage to those students who are drawn from uneducated homes, on the other hand, where colleges are brought within easy reach of day students' homes, the home influence acting side by side with that of the training college will be of great value. In recommending that facilities for the establishment of day training colleges should be afforded in one of the ways above mentioned, the Commission think that their government should be both of an educational and local character, and that no aid should be given them from the rates. They conclude their remarks on these proposals by reiterating their conviction that the present system of training colleges is the best both for teachers and scholars, and unanimously recommend only a limited system of day training to meet the cases of those for whom at present residence at a training college cannot be provided.

CHAPTER VII.

ATTENDANCE AND COMPULSION.

The Commission express great satisfaction at the striking increase in so short a time in the number of children brought into school under the provisions of the Acts of 1870, '76, and '80 as exhibited in the tables supplied by the Education Department and printed in the Appendix to the First Volume of the Report, which show that the number of scholars on the roll in elementary schools receiving grants had risen from 7·66 per cent. of the estimated population in 1870, to 16·24 per cent. in 1886.

Increase of scholars on the roll.

It is asserted by some witnesses that in many places practically all the school population is now on the roll of some efficient school.

Almost all children on the roll.

Regularity of attendance. The Commission also report that the number of registered scholars in average attendance has risen from 68·09 per cent. in 1870 to 76·27 in 1886, leaving room for considerable improvement, which is most likely to be found where a school is thoroughly good, and the buildings are attractive, and where the teachers interest themselves in the scholars out of school hours, as well as during school time.

Causes of improved regularity. Apart from compulsion—to which the great increase of the numbers on the roll is largely attributed—two causes which have tended to produce the improvement in attendance are noted in the Report, one being the value which parents who have been themselves educated attach to the discipline and education to be gained by the punctual attendance of their children; the other, the improvement in the homes and the increase in the comforts of the working classes, who have thus become more sensible of the ill-consequences of ignorance.

Compulsion. Passing on to the question of compulsion, the Commission say that though it is not altogether efficacious in securing regularity of attendance, yet it has contributed to increase the number of children attending school, first, by its direct influence over the parents in producing a fear of punishment; secondly, by its indirect influence, in that parents feel it a disgrace to be brought before a magistrate, and are made to recognize that the State regards it as a neglect of duty if their children remain uneducated; and thirdly, by the introduction of labour certificates, parents being anxious that their children should be exempt from school as soon as possible.

Expedients for improving The Report goes on to mention various expedients for promoting the regular attendance of different classes of children, such as the establishment of day industrial **regularity.** schools and of truant schools, under Lord Sandon's Act, and the offer of prizes for regular attendance, all of which are said to have had a good effect. The Commission however think that teachers and managers by their personal influence might secure still greater regularity, and that it is desirable to encourage parents to take a warmer interest in their children's instruction. This might be done in various ways, by sending them, for example, each year a report of the child's progress and conduct, and by encouraging scholars to take home their reading books and to read them aloud to their parents. It is thought also that if manual training were generally introduced, it would have the effect of inducing parents to increase their efforts to secure the regular attendance of their children, and to prolong their stay at school.

Many complaints, however, were made to the Com- **Local** mission, both by oral witnesses and in answer to statistical **authorities.** inquiries, as to the inaction and leniency of magistrates, the indifference of local authorities, and the inefficiency of attendance officers. In London, the Commission say, the number of School Board cases which can be heard in one day is so limited by the magistrates, that the working of the compulsory law seems to be seriously impeded. The suggestion, however, to appoint a special magistrate for London to adjudicate on school attendance cases, is regarded as objectionable in principle. With **Attendance** regard to the complaints of the unsuitability and inefficiency **officers.** of attendance officers, the Commission remark that the influence of the managers and a little special attention on the part of teachers, are in many cases as likely to secure regularity as the action of attendance officers; and they recommend that the latter should always be required to

D

furnish periodical returns of absentees from each school to the local authorities, who are the proper persons to decide the smallest number of attendances that shall be deemed **Local committees.** compliance with the letter of the bye-laws. The Commission also recommend as of great importance that local committees should be more generally appointed in each district under School Attendance Committees, as provided by Section 32 of the Act of 1876, who should deal with cases of irregularity on the spot, and that School Attendance Committees should hold meetings in different parts of their districts more generally accessible to the population. In considering the complaints against the local authorities, the Commission say that owing to the complex conditions of regularity of attendance, the comparative efficiency of **Comparison between School Boards and School Attendance Committees.** School Boards and School Attendance Committees in urban and rural districts respectively cannot with any certainty be estimated, though from a table taken from the Report of the Department for 1881-2, it appears that School Attendance Committees at that date showed more activity than rural School Boards in carrying out compulsion; at the same time it is remarked that many large School Boards look after the attendance with commendable vigour, special mention being made of Huddersfield.

Premature removal of children from school. Information comes from various quarters that a great majority of children leave school on passing the exemption standard, and lose quickly the small amount of knowledge they have acquired; reference, however, is made to a Return furnished by the Department, which shows for the years 1870, '75, '80, and '86, an appreciable increase in the percentage of scholars on the register over the ages of 10, 12, and 13 respectively, which the Commission find hard to reconcile with the statement that children leave school earlier than formerly. To check this alleged premature removal of children from school as soon as they are legally **Proposed remedies.** exempt, one remedy suggested by several witnesses was that of raising the minimum standard in all cases to the fifth; another was that of abolishing exemption standards and substituting an age standard. The Commission, however, **Half-time exemption in rural districts.** recognizing that in the case of children preparing for many employments (including agriculture) school life is often incompatible with early instruction of a practical nature, and also taking into consideration the poverty of large families in rural districts, are of opinion that, as already sanctioned by the 9th Section of the Act of 1876, children should be exempted from school attendance who are actually needed for *bonâ fide* employment in suitable farm work at busy seasons, but that they should attend regularly during the remainder of the year. Subject to this **Half-time exemption in urban districts.** recommendation as to rural districts, the further opinion is expressed that the minimum age for half-time exemption should be 11, and for full-time exemption 13.*

The Commission express surprise that the annual in- **Article 15 of Code of 1882.** structions to Inspectors do not now direct them to explain that Article 15 of the Code of 1882† provides for the partial exemption of those children only between 10 and 13 who, having passed the standard prescribed by the bye-laws of the district, are "beneficially and necessarily employed." The re-insertion therefore of this instruction is recommended, and the hope is expressed that when the Article is understood it will have as beneficial an effect on children employed in labour not regulated by an Act,

* Sir Francis Sandford objects to the minimum age of 11 for half-time, and 13 for full-time exemption, and would recommend instead Standard III or the age of 10 for partial exemption, and Standard V or the age of 14 for total exemption.

† Report of Committee of Council, 1885-6, Instructions to Inspectors, p. 166: "You should explain to the members of School Boards that a child is bound to attend school full-time whenever it is not *beneficially* and *necessarily* employed, and that a *bonâ-fide* half-timer means a child who is legally at work when not at school." D 2

as the Act of 1878 has on children employed in workshops and factories.

Employment of children at theatres. Adverting to the employment of children (about 1,000 in London) in theatres, and the bad effect it is said to have upon their health, morals, and education, the Commission recommend that the legal powers for dealing with this evil should be strengthened, and they are of opinion that one remedy would be to bring theatrical employment under the Factory Acts.

Summary of obstacles to school attendance. The obstacles to school attendance are thus summarised in the Report : 1. The desire of parents to profit by their children's labour. 2. The poverty of parents. 3. The indifference of parents to education. 4. Truancy. 5. Home needs. 6. Migration of families in the towns, and bad roads and weather in the country.

Demand for more stringent " compulsion." Special attention is drawn to the demands made for a more stringent system of compulsion by managers and teachers in their answers to the printed inquiries addressed to them, and although the Commission do not agree in condemning generally the administration of the compulsory bye-laws, they at the same time recognize that there are very considerable local shortcomings calling for amendment. They also express an opinion that the Department should exercise through their inspectors and by means of periodical returns constant vigilance over the action of local authorities in securing regular attendance, and should report at stated intervals to Parliament upon the subject. Although the demand made very generally by managers and teachers that the age and standard of partial and total exemption should be considerably raised, has not been complied with, it is thought that the consensus of opinion expressed will make it easier to carry out the alterations in the age of exemption suggested.

CHAPTER VIII.

RELIGIOUS AND MORAL TRAINING.

THE inquiry into the religious and moral training given in Importance of religious and moral elementary schools is prefaced in the Report with the training. statement that while the whole Commission are animated by the desire to secure for the children the best and most thorough instruction in secular subjects, they are also unanimously of opinion that their religious and moral training is a matter of still higher importance alike to the children themselves, their parents, and the nation at large. The Report goes on to say :—

> " We are persuaded that the only safe foundation on which to Chris-
> " construct a theory of morals, or to secure high moral conduct, tianity the basis of
> " is the religion which our Lord Jesus Christ has taught the moral teaching.
> " world. As we look to the Bible for instruction concerning
> " morals, and take its words for the declaration of what is
> " morality, so we look to the same inspired source for the
> " sanctions by which men may be led to practise what is there
> " taught, and for instruction concerning the help by which they
> " may be enabled to do what they have learned to be right."

Having quoted the evidence of several witnesses who Testimony of those in failed to see how the teaching of morals could be separated favour of religious from religious instruction, namely, the Rev. J. Duncan, education. Mr. Matthew Arnold, Canon Warburton, and the Rev. Dr. Richards, the Commission say that such seems to be also the opinion of the country at large, as appears by the fact that only very few school boards in England and Wales have dispensed entirely with religious teaching, and also by the great increase in the number of voluntary schools in which the whole basis of education is religious. They further say that the evidence is practically unanimous in showing the desire of the parents for the religious training of their children.

Religious instruction in board schools. Although the number of board schools which give no religious instruction is very small, it is reported that in not a few, as shown by the Parliamentary Returns, the provision for the religious training of the children is very meagre, such as reading the Bible without note or comment, or reciting the Lord's Prayer.

Its effect. The evidence shows that the estimate of the value and effects of the religious instruction given in board schools varies with the standpoint from which the several witnesses regard it, and the Commission say there is good ground for concluding that where care and time are bestowed on the religious teaching, it is of a nature to affect the conscience and influence the conduct of the children of whose daily training it forms a part.

The hope also is expressed that, in voluntary and board schools alike, the religious and moral training may be generally raised to the high standard already attained in many of them, and that it will be made clear that the State, while scrupulously safeguarding the rights of conscience, does not wish to discourage any endeavour made to bring up children in love and obedience to God. With **Parliamentary regulation of religious teaching.** regard to the Cowper-Temple clause of the Act of 1870,* the Commission say it does not appear in what other way the State could have disconnected itself from all distinctive religious teaching in elementary schools, nor can they concur in the view that the State may be constructively regarded as endowing religious education, when under the conditions of the Act of 1870 it pays annual grants for

---

* Section XIV, Act of 1870, prohibits the use of distinctive religious formularies in a rate-supported school.

secular instruction in voluntary schools in which religious
instruction is also carried on. Mention is here made of **Act of 1870,** what is thought to be a very prevalent misconception of **Section 7.**
Section 7 of the Act of 1870 as regards the meaning of
the conscience clause, and the evidence of two witnesses
is quoted which shows that a strained interpretation is put
upon the wording of the Act, when it is assumed to forbid
any appeal to Scripture or the mention of the name of
God during the hours of secular instruction. The Commission refer to Mr. Forster's assertion that it is the general
opinion of the enormous majority of the country that the
standard of right and wrong is based on religion, and to
his explicit refusal to alter the clause in order to prevent
the possibility of any allusion to religious subjects outside
the hours set apart for secular instruction.

The Commission say that under the 7th section what a
parent may claim for his child is exemption from "instruction in religious subjects," and that similarly in the
Endowed Schools Act, which Mr. Forster passed in 1869,
the teacher is forbidden "in the course of other lessons"
to teach "systematically and persistently any particular
religious doctrine" from the teaching of which exemption
has been claimed.

The statistical inquiries made in various counties and **Conscience**
districts, are said to prove clearly that the conscience **clause.**
clause is practically operative all over the country
in the most widely different classes and districts of the
population. In explanation of the small number of children
withdrawn from religious instruction, the Report says
that some witnesses assigned as the reason that parents
generally are fairly satisfied with the instruction given in
schools even of a different denomination from their own;
on the other hand it was alleged that they often forego

the right of withdrawing their children from religious instruction through fear of unpleasant consequences, although the Commission failed to find proof of the existence of any just grounds for this fear. At the same time, the importance of removing any impressions of unfair pressure exerted in the administration of the conscience clause is fully recognized.

Reference is made to the special provisions of the Act of 1876, section 7, and also to the instructions issued to H.M. Inspectors in 1878, with a view to secure the strict observance of the conscience clause, under which the local educational authority as well as H.M. Inspectors are bound to report to the Education Department any infraction of the provisions of Section 7 (*i.e.* the conscience clause) of the Act of 1870.

Hour of marking registers. Attention is drawn to the prevailing system of marking the registers after the religious teaching and observances. Two serious dangers are said thereby to arise: First, it causes the religious instruction to be considered of small importance; and secondly, the very children for whom such instruction would be of special value, will be most tempted not to attend until it is over. It is recommended therefore that all registers should be marked before the religious teaching and observances begin, the most scrupulous care being taken to provide for the case of children whose parents object to such teaching, in accordance with the spirit and letter of the conscience clause.

Proposal to prohibit religious instruction. The evidence of several witnesses is quoted who would prefer wholly secular schools, and do not shrink from urging that the State should prohibit all religious instruction in elementary schools, although many were still ready to acquiesce in the compromise of 1870, by which undenominational Biblical teaching was left to the discretion of the local representative authorities. In support of this contention it is urged that religious teaching makes an undesirable tax on the teacher's energies; though, on the other hand, experienced witnesses protested against its exclusion, on the ground that teachers themselves would object if they were debarred from giving religious and moral instruction, and that their influence would suffer by the omission. Effects on teachers.

As to the further objection that the use of the Bible as a school book is likely to lower it in the estimation of the scholars, the Commission received no evidence to show any grounds for such a fear, while they state their opinion that teachers have a special aptitude for giving religious instruction, since a very large proportion of them have been specially trained for this task. The Bible as a school book.

The evidence, it is asserted, shows conclusively how great a value parents set on the religious instruction given in the day school, and the Commission express their conviction that the secularization of elementary education by the State would be contrary to the wishes of parents, whose views on this matter are entitled to the first consideration. Assuming that parents are generally unable to undertake the religious education of their children, which is admitted even by those who favour secular schools, two plans were put forward for supplying religious instruction: either (i) by means of Sunday schools and other voluntary agencies, or (ii) by an organized system of religious instruction to be given daily in schools by volunteers, either before or after school hours. With regard to this latter proposal the evidence before the Commission did not satisfy them that children would voluntarily attend this supplementary instruction, and also failed to show from what source an efficient body of voluntary teachers could be Views of parents. Parents are unable to supply the void. Alternative proposals.

provided, and they cannot recommend the plan suggested as an efficient substitute for the present system, which appears to give general satisfaction to the parents.

As to the alternative plan, that of instruction in the Sunday school, and by other voluntary agencies, the evidence shows that, in large towns at least, many day scholars do not regularly attend Sunday schools, the majority of absentees belonging naturally to the neglected classes who especially require to be brought under religious influences.

Diocesan Inspection. Comparing the result of the religious instruction at the present time with what it was at an earlier period, the Commission report that it is as good now in voluntary schools as it was before the Act of 1870, if not much better, chiefly owing to the system of diocesan inspection. The need of some examination into the religious instruction given in board schools, of a kind similar to the diocesan inspection, was recognized by the representatives of many boards. And the Commission think that the same facilities for setting apart a day for such inspection should be given by law to School Boards as is allowed by the Act of 1870, section 76,* to the managers of voluntary schools.

Moral discipline. In pursuance of that clause of the Code which requires H.M. Inspectors to report on the discipline of a school, the Commission have no evidence to show whether as a rule they do more than observe any indications of the moral tone that may occur during the examination, but the abolition of the clause is not recommended, since it serves to remind those who conduct schools of the importance attached by the State to moral training.

Recommendations as to moral training. The Commission accordingly make the following recommendation as regards moral training in schools :—

---

* Act of 1870, Sec. 76, allows an examination of voluntary schools in religious knowledge, on one or two days, after notice.

" We are strongly of opinion that much greater support should
" be given by the State to the moral element of training in
" our schools, almost the only reference to such matters as
" far as the State is concerned, being that under the head
" of Discipline in the Code, which, being only introduced in
" 1876, has already been once withdrawn by the Department
" in 1882, and may be removed in any year. We recom-
" mend, therefore, that general fundamental and fixed
" instructions should be laid down as to moral training,
" making it an essential condition of the efficiency of a
" public elementary school that it should be held to
" comprise such matters as instruction in duty and
" reverence to parents, honour and truthfulness in word
" and act, honesty, purity, temperance, consideration and
" respect for others, obedience, cleanliness, good manners,
" duty to country, the discouragement of bad language,
" and the like.

" And as we have found with regret that in recent years this
" branch of the inspectors' duty has not received the attention
" it deserved, we therefore think it necessary to make it a
" distinct recommendation that it should be considered the
" first duty of Her Majesty's inspectors to inquire into and
" report upon the moral training and condition of the schools
" under the various heads set forth above, and to impress
" upon the managers, teachers, and children the primary
" importance of this essential element of all education."

After hearing the arguments with respect to a wholly Conclu-
secular education, the Commission come to the following
conclusions :—

" (1.) That it is of the highest importance that all children
" should receive religious and moral training.

" (2.) That the evidence does not warrant the conclusion that
" such religious and moral training can be amply provided
" otherwise than through the medium of elementary schools.

" (3.) That in schools of a denominational character to which
" parents are compelled to send their children, the parents

" have a right to require an operative conscience clause, so
" that care be taken that the children shall not suffer in any
" way in consequence of their taking advantage of the
" conscience clause.

" (4.) That inasmuch as parents are compelled to send their
" children to school, it is just and desirable that, as far as
" possible, they should be enabled to send them to a
" school suitable to their religious convictions or
" preferences."

" (5.) We also are of opinion that it is of the highest import-
" ance that the teachers who are charged with the moral
" training of the scholars should continue to take part in the
" religious instruction. We should regard any separation
" of the teacher from the religious teaching of the school
" as injurious to the morals and secular training of the
" scholars."

CHAPTER IX.

CURRICULUM OF INSTRUCTION.

Scope of the Inquiry. THE Commission state that they have endeavoured to ascertain what are the results obtained under the present curriculum, and also how far it is adapted to the several kinds of elementary schools, and to the varying ages and conditions of the scholars attending them. They call attention to the fact that witnesses of all classes have testified to the imperfect hold which the knowledge gained in school seems to have upon the scholars, and say that if this is the case with reading, writing, and arithmetic, which all children to a certain extent keep in practice, it is to be feared that the knowledge of other subjects to which they have given their attention evaporates even more quickly.

To remedy this evil they are of opinion that "a thorough grounding in knowledge is essential in any national system," and that "to teach a child to observe and think by proper training of the mind will more effectually develop its capacity and faculties than premature initiation into matters beyond its intellectual habits."

The evidence against the present system of standards **The standards.** is referred to at some length, the chief objections urged being that it hinders the clever, over-presses the dull, and produces bad classification. Mr. Matthew Arnold, the Report says, would have abolished the standards, and in their place would have recommended that, after the example of other countries, the work of each class and the hours devoted to each subject should be rigidly prescribed, the books approved by the Department, and above all that the teachers should be better trained.

Mr. Sharpe, on the other hand, regards the standards as good for large schools, but considers that more elasticity is needed for small schools; while Mr. Fitch would dispense with the recording of individual passes in Standards I and II, and would examine individually in Standards III, IV, V, and VI, paying the full grant for 75 per cent. of passes. On the whole the Commission **Conclusion.** think that the standards are too valuable to be abolished, but that they should be carefully revised with a view to some modifications in the method of examination and in their grouping, especially in small schools. They are also of opinion that perfect freedom in the classification of scholars according to their abilities should be permitted.*

* Mr. Alderson opposes the retention of the present system of standards, as being "a scheme of education which is at once depressing and sterile," and one which destroys rational classification; he would, however, use the standards for the purpose of passing children to labour, and would transfer their administration *ad hoc* to the local or county inspector, "who," as Mr. Alderson puts it, "fell still-born from the report of the Duke of Newcastle's Commission."

Elementary subjects, reading. Coming next to the elementary subjects, complaints appear to be numerous that the quality of the reading is too mechanical and unintelligent, that the books are dry and not written in the language of the children's home-life, that they are too few in number, and that the reading lesson is interrupted with spelling instead of being wholly devoted to reading and the giving of proper expression. The Commission recognize that there is room for much improvement in reading, and recommend an increase in the number of books for each standard, with diminished requirements for spelling, and that teachers should try to secure fluency and expression by reading aloud themselves to the scholars; they also think it would be well for the Department to consider whether the reading of Shakespeare's historical plays in Standard VI, and of Shakespeare and Milton in Standard VII, should continue to be **School libraries.** enforced. The establishment of school libraries as an encouragement to home reading is strongly recommended.

Writing and spelling. Little is said as to writing and spelling, except that too much attention is paid to the latter art, which is believed to come often unconsciously, by the practice of reading, and that handwriting would improve if drawing were universally taught.

Arithmetic. With regard to arithmetic, the Report quotes the evidence of one witness who thinks that too much is required in the higher standards, the transition between Standards III and IV being too great; of another who desires to see fractions introduced earlier; of a third who speaks of the numbers dealt with as being too large, and the examination cards too difficult; and Mr. Oakeley, though not agreeing with these contentions, thinks certain modifica- **Recommendation.** tions are necessary. The Commission are of opinion that the schedule of arithmetic requires careful re-consideration, so that the standards may be suitably graduated to scholars of both sexes; that for the higher classes there should be a choice of practical rules to meet the industrial require- ments of different districts, and that inspectors should see that the principles of the rules have been taught as well as their actual application. A further recommendation is made, that the schedule of arithmetic for girls should be modified, since a large part of the time which boys are able to give to arithmetic is occupied by girls with needle- work.

Before proceeding to the class subjects, the Commission **Code syllabus.** make some suggestions with regard to the difficulty ex- perienced in preparing scholars for examination owing to the indefiniteness of the Code syllabus, and they think this defect will best be met by encouraging managers and teachers to avail themselves of the provision of the Code which enables them, with the approval of H.M. Inspector, to substitute for the Code syllabus a different scheme of instruction. They further recommend that alternative courses should be provided, and precisely defined in the Code, of which the one best suited to a school may be selected; so that by making the instruction more interest- ing, and by framing syllabuses in later standards so as to recapitulate the lessons already learnt, the knowledge which children have once acquired may not be so easily forgotten.

A suggestion that there should be a set of text books **Official text books.** recognized by Government, meets with no favour from the Commission, though it is thought it would be expedient to indicate to managers and teachers within what limits the official examination will be confined, by publishing a more or less extended programme for each subject, such as is adopted in the Science and Art Directory, which would not only provide against an overloaded curriculum, but would also be very valuable in helping teachers to adapt their lessons to the capacities and circumstances of their scholars.

It is especially remarked that definite programmes of studies are required for pupil-teachers, to guide the examiners in framing appropriate questions for the Queen's Scholarship examinations.

Class subjects, English. The Report says complaints are made that English as a class subject, where any are taken, ought not to be obligatory, since history and geography are thereby set aside. The Commission are of opinion that this provision of the Code should be repealed, and that the Department might well consider whether a reference to any special authors in the Code might not be omitted. It is further said that the technical grammar is too dry, and the requirements excessive; though on the other hand some witnesses consider grammar and analysis too valuable to be left out where two class subjects are taken.

The advantage of learning English poetry by heart is strongly advocated, and while the retention of parsing and analysis is recommended, the exercises of word-building and Latin prefixes, it is thought, might be left to the teacher's discretion.

Geography. Special mention is made of the excellence of the geography as taught in elementary schools, whilst the systematic teaching of history, owing to its restriction to the fifth and higher Standards, is practically discouraged; and it is suggested that the inspectors should require a knowledge of the subject matter of the historical reading book. For geography a more exact definition of the requirements of the Code is asked for, embracing for Standard VII some particular part of the present very comprehensive course, and it is recommended that an alternative syllabus should be included in the Code.

The Commission think that the Code should contain a **History.** syllabus for history, and while recognizing the impossibility of completing in an elementary school a course of constitutional history, they recommend in Standards VI and VII the acquirement of some knowledge of our constitution and national institutions. Finally they express their desire to see children grounded in all four class subjects, or, if this be not feasible, to leave the selection between them to the school authorities.

Proceeding next to consider the specific subjects, **Specific** although it is recognized that they are incapable of uni- **subjects,** versal application, the practical value of domestic economy **economy** is regarded as demanding special consideration, and **physiology.** instruction in the elementary principles of physiology as likely to be of advantage to girls in after life.

In dealing with the bi-lingual difficulty in Wales, it is **Welsh** stated that complaints are made that Welsh children are **and the** treated by the Code as if they always spoke English, **difficulty.** whereas the bulk of them come to school wholly ignorant of it, so that the English acquired at school is superficial and in a great measure soon lost. Witnesses from Wales contended that Welsh schools should be allowed to teach, at the discretion of the managers, reading and writing in the vernacular together with English, and the Commission say that permission to use bi-lingual reading books would meet the objection that too much reading matter has to be prepared in Welsh schools.

They also think there is good reason for making the following concessions to the Welsh-speaking population the recognition in the Code of Welsh as a specific subject; the adoption of a graduated system of translation from

Welsh to English to meet the present requirements of English grammar; the teaching of Welsh along with English as a class subject; and the inclusion of Welsh among the languages in which candidates for Queen's Scholarships and certificates of merit may be examined.

Drawing. A recommendation is made in this chapter with regard to drawing, although the subject is more fully dealt with in the chapter on Technical Instruction. The drawing schedule, it is said, is too difficult, and consequently instruction in this subject in village schools is practically discouraged. Great value is attached to drawing in the evidence referred to, one witness describing it as "the best kind of technical education at present available;" another as "the foundation of all industrial pursuits;" and the Commission agree in regarding drawing as a most important subject, the teaching of which in England is inferior to that in other countries; they recommend that for boys it should be made compulsory, and although difficulties exist in the way of making the same recommendation with regard to girls, they point out that in many employments girls would find an elementary knowledge of the subject of great practical utility. To meet the difficulty of providing instruction in drawing in rural districts, it is thought that possibly itinerant teachers, duly qualified, might be able to conduct it in a group of schools.

Object lessons. It is suggested that object lessons on elementary science in the lower standards of schools for older children given in sequence to those of the infant school, would facilitate science teaching in the upper standards. The Commission concur in the recommendation of the Royal Commission on Technical Instruction, that geography should be regarded as a branch of elementary science, that it should be taught by means of object lessons varying with the circumstances of each locality, and further they say it must not be learnt by books but by oral illustration.

The progress in "Needlework" is favourably reported Needle-work. on, and the hope is expressed that sustained efforts will continue to be made to teach this subject practically and efficiently.

Of "Cookery" also good results are reported, so far as Cookery. it has been carried—especially under the London School Board—and the Commission think that the Department should aim at removing within a reasonable period the existing difficulties of expense and organization, in order that a system of lessons adapted to good and economical cottage cookery may be more widely provided.

As to teaching music, the continued payment of 6d. Music. per head for singing by ear meets with approval, since to recognize only the higher step of singing by note would, it is thought, lead in many schools to musical training being abandoned.

The Commission think that the want of physical training Physical calls for serious consideration, the number of rejected army training. candidates, as shown by War Office statistics, pointing to alarming inferiority in the physical development of boys, especially those from urban districts, where from the scarcity and limited area of playgrounds some system of physical training would be very valuable both for mind and body. The training colleges however are looked to for the introduction of a safe and scientific system of physical training, and special certificates, it is recommended, should be given to teachers duly qualified to conduct it.

On the subject of the elementary curriculum, the Limits of Commission say that, as the meaning and limits of the elementary education

E 2

yet to be defined. term *elementary* have not been defined in the Education Acts, nor by any judicial or authoritative interpretation, but depend only upon the annual Codes of the Department, on whose power of framing such Codes no limit has hitherto been imposed, it would appear to be of absolute necessity that some definition of the instruction to be paid for out of the rates and taxes should be put forth by the Legislature, and that, until this is done, the limits of primary and secondary education cannot be defined.

Conclusion. The Commission conclude by expressing their opinion that the quality of education would be improved if the Code contained several schemes of instruction, so as to allow managers to introduce a curriculum into their schools suited to the character and requirements of their respective localities; at the same time they strongly emphasise their sense of the necessity of looking to the quality at least as much as to the extent of the instruction given.

The following are regarded as subjects essential to elementary instruction, due regard being paid to the qualifications already made :—

Reading.	English, so as to give the
Writing.	children an adequate know-
Arithmetic.	ledge of their mother
Needlework (for girls).	tongue.
Linear drawing (for boys).	English history, taught by means of reading books.
Singing.	

Geography, especially of the British Empire.

Lessons on common objects in the lower standards, leading up to a knowledge of elementary science in the higher standards.

CHAPTER X.

MANUAL AND TECHNICAL INSTRUCTION.

TECHNICAL instruction is defined in the Report as **Definition.** "instruction in those scientific or artistic principles which "underlie the industrial occupations of the people (includ- "ing especially handicrafts, manufactures, mining and "agricultural labour), as well as instruction in the manual "practice involved in the application of such principles."

The Commission, after recording the recent changes **Drawing.** that have occurred in the control of the instruction in drawing, which was for a short time transferred from the Science and Art, to the Education, Department, and shortly afterwards was re-transferred to the Science and Art Department, recommend that drawing should, as far as practicable, be made a compulsory subject in all boys' schools; and, under suitable conditions, should be encouraged amongst girls. (See page 50.)

With regard to elementary science it is said to be **Elementary science.** still in its infancy, and scarcely ever taught in the lower standards of an elementary school. The evidence of Sir Henry Roscoe is quoted to the effect that science teaching in this country is much below what it ought to be, and below that given on the Continent; and of Mr. Balchin, who says that the present school training fits for the office rather than for the workshop. The Commission express their concurrence in these views, and consider that scholars will best be fitted to fulfil their respective duties in life, and to develop the special gifts with which each is endowed, by some *elementary* instruction in mathematical, mechanical, and physical science, a subject only second in importance to the three elementary subjects, and which is regarded not only as the foundation, but as an essential part, of thorough technical instruction.

Science teaching. The testimony of several witnesses is referred to, the majority of whom are decidedly in favour of giving some manual and technical instruction to boys in elementary schools. The Commission specially urge in connection with science teaching: (i) That care must be taken that by its too early introduction in the school life it does not interfere with the general instruction; and (ii) That good science teaching cannot for obvious reasons be expected of the ordinary elementary master. This want of the necessary qualification has led, it is said, to the practice with some boards, notably those of Liverpool, Birmingham, and **Itinerant science teacher.** London, of employing an itinerant science teacher who goes from school to school, teaching boys in the presence of their master. From the reports of the several examiners employed by the Boards, and here referred to, it appears that such an arrangement has worked successfully, and that the examinations are considered of great value, though the Commission, having received no evidence on the point, are unable to express an opinion as to the lasting character of the results obtained. With regard to the examinations in science it is recommended that, as far as possible, they should be conducted orally and not on paper, especially in the first five standards.

Manual and technical instruction. The evidence is said to show undoubtedly a desire among many managers and teachers that some practical instruction in industries and the use of tools should be given in elementary schools; but the Commission are of opinion that it should not be applicable to boys under 10 years of age, though they think it would be of advantage if some judicious systematised science teaching were given to the younger scholars, as for instance collecting and preparing specimens, and helping to make models in their geography lessons, as illustrated in the evidence of Mr. Balchin and Mr. Wilks.

The following passage in Sir Philip Magnus' evidence is quoted as fairly indicating what should be the proper aim in the matter; he said :—

" I have suggested that drawing should be taught generally in
" our public elementary schools; that more attention should
" be devoted to the teaching of science than at present is
" given to it; that handicraft instruction should be intro-
" duced after a certain standard."
" I think that further encouragement should be given to
"instruction in evening schools, in order that the children
" may not forget the knowledge and the skill which they
" have acquired in the elementary schools, and which they
" will need to apply when they come to take advantage of
" the excellent science, art, and technical classes which are
" now organized in different parts of the country."

It is recognized that as small rural schools must be content with a more limited range of studies, so the complete realization even of those aims must be gradual, and must be the result of improved qualifications in teachers, and improvement in their methods of instruction. *Small rural schools.*

It is recommended that in order to give children better manual instruction than can be provided in the elementary school, a workshop should be established in connection with some higher institution, where such is within reach, for desirable boys of exceptional ability, and that the time spent at the central school on one or two afternoons a week should count as attendance at the elementary school. It is further proposed that such a workshop, if thought desirable by the local authority, should be established and maintained as if it were a technical school. *A workshop available for element-ary scholars.*

Scholars not sufficiently prepared for higher technical instruction. The Commission here observe that many witnesses who gave evidence before them, as well as before the Technical Commission, testified to the greater benefit which would be derived by scholars if they were better prepared on leaving school to profit by the higher technical instruction provided by the Science and Art Department or the City and Guilds of London Technical Institute; and this the Commission say is an additional argument for the more general introduction of drawing and elementary science into our elementary schools.

The money difficulty. With regard to the extra cost of technical instruction in elementary schools, and especially in voluntary schools, the Commission are of opinion that voluntary schools may fairly expect liberal public aid in order to enable them to supply technical instruction on a footing of equality with board schools, since this form of instruction was not contemplated at the time when Mr. Forster's Act was passed. At the same time as a guarantee to the State that those subjects are taught which are suited to the wants of the locality, and not such as might be taken up only to obtain **Provisos.** the additional grant, the following provisos are suggested as necessary, namely, that some proportion of the cost of supplying suitable technical instruction in elementary schools should be thrown upon the local rates; that grants to managers of voluntary schools in which efficient elementary technical instruction is given should be partially met by contributions from the rates of the district in which the schools are situated; that it should be the duty of the Department to define the subjects, and the maximum number that may be taught; and that no grants from the rates shall be made to voluntary schools for subjects that are not taught in one or more board schools of the district, or which are not declared by the rating authority as needful to the educational requirements of the district.

In connection with advanced technical instruction and its relation to elementary schools, attention is drawn to a passage in the Report of the Technical Commission which states that undoubtedly our nation still maintains its position at the head of the industrial world, notwithstanding that foreigners are making every effort by means of the widespread establishment of technical schools to surpass us; an argument, the Commission say, for the introduction into England of a general system of technical instruction, such as is in vogue on the continent. *Advanced technical instruction.*

A full description is given of the method employed at Birmingham in working what is called a Seventh Standard School. To this school it appears only those scholars are admitted who have passed Standard VI. The subjects taught besides the three elementary subjects are machine construction, chemistry, and electricity; the instruction given is laid out for a course of three years, a practical mechanic being employed to superintend the workshop teaching. The Commission however think that this system, if much further developed, would lead to the creation of practically secondary schools, where the children of wealthier parents would be educated at the public cost. *Seventh standard school at Birmingham.*

Whilst acknowledging the great work already done in the direction of technical instruction, the Commission are of opinion that it is now time to consider whether further help should not be given from public sources, and whether some local public body should be empowered to provide for or contribute towards the maintenance of technical schools suited to different localities. In carrying this into effect, precautions, it is said, should be taken: (i) that voluntary effort shall not thereby be discouraged; (ii) that *Recommendations.*

the school shall not supersede the workshop; (iii) that technical schools shall only be established where they are shown to be necessary.

The control of technical instruction. With regard to the control of technical instruction, the Commission recommend that the Education Department should supervise its management, and not the Science and Art Department, South Kensington. It is also thought desirable that the central authority in London should not interfere with the various methods of promoting technical instruction, so long as those methods are adapted to the circumstances of different localities. Further, they express the opinion that—

> " Where there are municipalities . . . . . the local
> " control of technical education should be lodged in their
> " hands; in other places it should be exercised by the rating
> " authorities. The national and imperial character of London,
> " the conditions of its organizations and industry, and the
> " absence at present of any central municipal authority, will
> " require exceptional treatment."

Oversight of technical schools The immediate oversight and direction of such schools, it is recommended, should be placed in the hands of a board of management of those who are interested and experienced in the local industries; and that while these schools should as far as possible be made self-supporting by fees, if necessary, where sufficient local interest is proved to exist, local resources might be aided by a contribution from the Parliamentary grant.

CHAPTER XI.

VARIOUS CLASSES OF ELEMENTARY SCHOOLS.

THE Commission recall the fact that previous to the *Origin of board schools.* Act of 1870, which established the School Board system, nearly all elementary schools were voluntary, many being supported wholly by fees and subscriptions. They report that since 1870 4,402 board schools have sprung up, about a quarter of which have been transferred by voluntary managers.

In comparing the relative efficiency of the board and *Relative efficiency of board and voluntary schools.* voluntary schools. attention is drawn to the material advantages that board schools have over voluntary schools. They have a larger purse to draw from, and therefore as a rule better buildings, furniture, and play-grounds, together with larger staffs; being for the most part situated in populous districts they are able to obtain a larger attendance than voluntary schools, many of which are conducted in thinly populated districts, though these frequently enjoy the advantage of close personal over-sight by the managers. The Commission remark that probably the truth is best expressed in the language of the witness who said, " The results are higher, taking them all round, in board schools ; but many of the best schools are not board schools."

Some witnesses, the Report says, advocated the aboli- *Abolition of voluntary schools.* tion of voluntary schools and the universal establishment of board schools, on the ground that voluntary schools are prevented from becoming really efficient through want of better support; they also urged that the system of voluntary schools is wrong in principle, that the board schools are necessary to protect religious liberty and are preferred by the working classes. On the other side it is contended that great advantages result from the healthy rivalry between the two classes of schools; that the rates would largely increase; that the abolition of voluntary schools would tend to secularise our system of education, and that to leave the various denominations to provide religious instruction outside the school would prove a failure. Some further point out that the abolition of voluntary schools would be a breach of faith with their managers, and that to compel people to support a system of which they disapprove would be a violation of religious **Conclusion.** liberty. The Commission, after weighing all the evidence, are of opinion that the State should continue to recognize both voluntary and board schools as constituent elements of national education, and that they should continue to share the benefits of the Parliamentary grant on an equal footing.

Small rural schools. To meet the difficulties experienced in small rural schools, the Report refers to the recommendations made in another chapter for the extension of special grants to them. (See page 77.)

The slender resources of small rural schools frequently result, the Report says, in undue economy in their management, and in a consequently insufficient staff; and the case is mentioned of a school taught by one mistress, with an average attendance of 60 children requiring as many as 31 separate lessons to be given daily. This difficulty, it is said, touches also small board schools, and statistics as to the high school board rates paid in districts with small populations suffice to show how heavily the burden of their maintenance weighs on the ratepayers.

The Report gives in detail the evidence of the Rev. Prebendary Roe (who spoke as to the financial conditions of small rural schools in Somersetshire, in districts having populations ranging from 90 to 500), showing that in 151 such schools each child costs the locality, on an average, 5s. 8d. a year more than the average cost in all Church of England schools, and that too with the help in many cases of the special grant which the Education Department was empowered in the Code of 1875 to make of £10 (or £15) to the only school available for a population not exceeding 300 (or 200). The Commission therefore come to the conclusion that local supporters are in such cases often over-burdened by the circumstances under which they have to meet the requirements of the Education Code. Nor does the evidence give any ground for hoping that the grant might be increased by an improved average attendance in these schools. An analysis of the items of grants received by these 151 schools shows how few have any instruction in the class subjects, or obtain the 1s. grant for singing. Prebendary Roe urged that the comparative meagreness of the grant earned in these schools was attributable to the lack of a proper staff, and said that with few exceptions managers were desirous of improving the staff if the conditions of the Code were altered. The Commission are strongly of opinion that a larger and in many cases a better staff ought to be provided for these small rural schools, and that the difficulty should be met by the extension of the system of special grants as hereinafter proposed. Further, they desire that not only should the additional teaching staff be provided by this increased grant, but also that the existing abnormal pressure on small schools should be thereby relieved.

Half-time schools.

As regards half-time schools, the Report says that half-time employment outside the Factory Acts is not on the increase, nor is the number of purely half-time schools very large. Some teachers are said to be opposed to the system on the ground that it is neither intellectually nor morally satisfactory. Other witnesses contend that the requirements of the Code are too exacting in demanding the same amount of work from half-timers as from whole-timers where both classes attend the same school. A suggestion was made by Sir Lovelace Stamer to the effect that it would be a great thing if half-timers could somehow be required to attend an evening school. The statistical inquiries are also said to show a disapproval of the system of half-time by managers and teachers, especially in the rural districts.

Workhouse and district schools, and pauper children in public elementary schools.

In workhouse schools, it is said, a want of intelligence in the children's knowledge of their subjects is shown; the industrial training is also said to be deficient, while in district poor-law schools the results obtained are better, owing to their having a somewhat more highly qualified staff. The intellectual education of pauper children attending public elementary schools is found to be very satisfactory, although difficulty arises in the management of the children out of school hours, and the time available for their industrial training is said to be too limited. The Commission think that the recommendations of the Industrial Schools Commission to transfer to the Education Department the educational inspection of reformatory, industrial, day industrial, and truant schools, might well be extended to workhouse schools.

Evening schools.

In considering the question of evening schools, the Commission agree with the witness who advocated the spending of more money by the State in this direction, in order "to keep up the cultivation of the intellectual faculty, and to carry it forward till it bears a fruitful result." But although numerous witnesses spoke of the necessity and value of evening schools, the evidence testifies to their gradual decay as an educational institution. This is attributed to insufficient encouragement from the Education Department, to the lack of freedom of classification, and to the absence of elasticity in the curriculum. The evidence goes to show that in towns a higher class of evening schools is required than in the country, and it is contended that these should be continuation schools where the formal teaching of the three standard subjects is omitted. *Causes of failure.*

Several witnesses directed attention to the value of the moral influence produced by evening schools, some of whom also urged the importance of introducing physical training as a part of the curriculum. The Commission express their full agreement that the retention of some educative and controlling influence over the scholars after leaving the day school would have an excellent moral effect; they also think the development of the physical powers of both sexes of the highest importance, and therefore recommend that physical as well as moral training should have a prominent position in the future curriculum of evening and continuation schools. *Moral effect of evening schools.*

It is said that witnesses generally regarded the question of the attendance of girls at evening schools with distavour upon moral grounds; the Commission however think that this must be a question for each locality, as in many places respectable girls are habitually out of doors in the evening when they might therefore be at school. *Should girls attend evening schools.*

With regard to any difficulty that may arise in con- *The annual*

**examina-
tion of
evening
schools.**
nection with the annual examination of evening schools, where it is impossible, by grouping or otherwise, to make up the number (20) of evening scholars now required to be presented in order to claim a separate examination, it is thought that there will be little difficulty in arranging for the examination of evening scholars, without requiring them, as at present, to be examined with the day scholars at their annual inspection.

**Who are
to be the
teachers.**
A difficulty is found in indicating the source from which the teachers in evening schools are to be drawn, and in acknowledging the valuable work done hitherto by voluntary workers, it is thought that in rural districts the instruction must still largely depend upon volunteers, but that in towns an organized staff of trained teachers might be supported at a moderate cost from the ranks of those who have married or quitted the teaching profession.

Conclusion.
The Commission upon the whole are decidedly of opinion that it would be worth the while of the State to spend more money on evening schools, and that the system should be thoroughly revised; that special schedules of standards and subjects should be permitted, adapted to different localities; and that local managers should be encouraged to submit such schedules to the Department for approval; that the provision in the present Code requiring all scholars to pass in reading, writing, and arithmetic, as a condition to the taking of additional subjects should cease to be enforced; and that no maximum limit of age should be imposed on the scholars.

While great freedom, the Commission say, should be given to managers and teachers, ample securities ought to be taken for the efficiency of such schools, so that more might be given as a fixed grant, and less as the

result of individual examination; and they are of opinion
that evening schools should in future be organized chiefly
with a view to continue and extend the curriculum of the
day school.

<hr/>

CHAPTER XII.

ELEMENTARY SCHOOLS AND HIGHER EDUCATION.

THE first question dealt with under this heading is the **Grouping of small schools.** possibility of reducing the number of small rural schools.
Although witnesses strongly recommended some system
of grouping small schools, the Commission say that the
evidence was not favourable to the proposal for the establishment of joint schools for several parishes, but they
think that individual cases may exist where it might be
advisable, for the better instruction of the older scholars;
they are unable, however, to recommend any general
system of grouping schools.

Whether it is desirable, and if so, under what circum- **Grading of schools.** stances, to grade the schools in large places, and to have
promotions from one to another, Mr. Matthew Arnold,
amongst other witnesses, was opposed to any such scheme,
being desirous of seeing the establishment of a system of
State-aided secondary education as more likely to
serve the desired object. Several other witnesses
also deprecated any such general proposal; Mr. Hance
gave it as his opinion that in thus seeking to promote the
higher education of the few, there would be great danger
of the general education of the mass being deteriorated.
The advocates of some system of grading or classifying

F

schools are, however, very numerous, and amongst the proposed schemes mentioned in the Report is one that is being gradually introduced at Salford, namely, a lower school for Standards I, II, and III, a middle school for Standards IV, V, and VI, and a higher school for Standards V, VI, and VII.

Conclusion. The Commission have little doubt but that, if due precautions are taken that all who would be likely to profit by the teaching in higher schools shall have an opportunity of being promoted to them, some system of grading might be of real advantage to the progress of elementary education in certain great centres of population.

Higher elementary schools. As to the character of the most advanced grade of primary schools, generally known as "higher elementary schools," on the one hand it was urged that they would be injurious to the ordinary elementary schools in drawing away the best children, that they would increase the charge on the rates, and that a system of secondary education would be preferable. On the other hand it was contended that the removal of the more forward children into one department would secure better classification, and that the system from an educational point of view had great advantages, and would be useful in providing well-prepared pupil-teachers.

A brief description of such higher schools in Huddersfield, Sheffield, Bradford, Birmingham, and Manchester, shows great diversity of type and constitution, the curriculum being generally regulated by the Code requirements up to Standard VII, and beyond that by the syllabus of the Science and Art Department.

Cost. Although in many instances these higher elementary schools cost little or nothing to the ratepayers, the Commission point out that besides the cost to the public of the Government Grants which they receive, and which are paid out of the Consolidated Fund, the interest on the money spent in the cost of buildings erected out of the rates ought also to be reckoned as a burden on the rates.

The evidence is said to be abundant in favour of the **Higher elementary schools and secondary schools.** popularity and general success of "higher elementary schools," which appear to be meeting the actual wants of more people than secondary schools, chiefly because they are cheaper, but opinions are much divided as to the policy of extending, or even continuing, them. The Commission remark that however desirable such schools may be, the principle involved should, if approved, be avowedly adopted, since their indirect inclusion in our educational system is injurious to both primary and secondary instruction. Still they are of opinion that so long as the **Conclusion.** curriculum does not invade the ground properly belonging to secondary education, and the promising children of poor parents are not excluded from them, higher elementary schools may prove a useful addition to our machinery for primary education. Further it is suggested that the **The curriculum.** object of such schools might in many cases be advanced by attaching to an ordinary school a class for those scholars who had passed Standard VII; the Commission also think that, as is already the case in Scotland, special grants for such higher instruction might be made to managers who provide it in their schools.

The present position of this class of schools is not con- **Present position of higher elementary schools.** sidered satisfactory, because the curriculum has to be adapted to meet the requirements of the Code, and because there is a tendency to provide, at the public cost, schools for children whose parents are able to pay fees sufficiently high to cover the expense of their education.

To meet these difficulties the Commission think that the State should in future to a greater extent than has been hitherto done draw a line between elementary and secondary education.

Difficulty of the maintenance of exhibitioners. A very general feeling is said to exist in favour of the adoption of some system of exhibitions or scholarships from elementary to higher or secondary schools; though it is contended that many poor children are unable to take advantage of such exhibitions, since they are usually only sufficient to pay the tuition fees.

Reference is made to a Return prepared by the Charity Commissioners, giving a list of about 1,000 schemes under the Charitable Trust and Endowed Schools Acts now in operation, the object of this return being to apprise the district inspector of all cases in which endowments are applicable to the promotion of scholars in or from the elementary schools which he visits, so that the inspector being officially cognisant of the means of secondary instruction in the district, may advise managers and parents to avail themselves of such opportunities for promising scholars.

Conclusion. The Commission having fully considered the means at present available to enable scholars to proceed to higher grade schools, come to the conclusion that first of all a supply of satisfactory secondary schools should be established and made adequate to meet the wants of all parts of the country, and secondly that increased funds are required in order to create sufficient exhibitions for deserving elementary scholars needing further instruction at those schools.

CHAPTER XIII.

GOVERNMENT EXAMINATION.

WITH respect to the Government examination, the Commission make some observations upon the great influence which the inspection day exercises on the whole work of a school, and though fully recognizing its value in keeping all concerned well up to their duty, they express some doubt as to whether the system fosters a healthy feeling under present conditions. *Examination day.*

Thus the Commission think that the examination very greatly affects the classification and teaching; in confirmation of which, reference is made to the evidence before them as to the rigidity of the present method of classification, which so far limits the freedom of organization, that as a consequence quick and clever children are kept back, and dull ones unduly pressed forward, a system unfair alike to teachers and children, and a waste of time and labour. *Its effects on the classification and teaching.*

It is said that witnesses do not agree as to whether the Department, through the inspectors, interferes in the organization of schools, but it is considered by the Commission that there is an indirect interference exercised in that children detained during a second year in the standard which they have passed inflict on the managers the same loss as if they had failed in all the subjects. *Departmental interference.*

To meet these complaints the Commission propose that if grants continue to be made on the principles of the existing Code, managers and teachers should be allowed full liberty of classification, subject to a reduction of grant if this liberty is abused, while small schools should be permitted to adopt a simpler classification both for instruction and examination. *Proposed remedies.*

Attendance qualification.

With regard to the change made by Mr. Mundella's Code in substituting the "22 weeks on the register" instead of "250 attendances" as the qualification for examination, the evidence before the Commission appears on the whole to show that the new regulation does not improve attendance, many teachers saying that irregularity is more prevalent than under the old rule, others that the temptation to falsify the registers is not altogether removed. The Commission are however of opinion that, if the present system is continued, every child might well be examined, and that the inspector should be directed to make allowance for any circumstances affecting the children and the school.

Individual examination.

Attention is called to the objections urged against the system of individual examination, namely, that it unnerves the children and engrosses too much of the inspector's time, and the Commission think that while in Standards I and II class examination might take the place of the present individual examination, from Standard III individual passes should continue to be recorded, as a guide to managers and teachers as well as parents. It is also pointed out that whatever changes may be effected in the system of paying the grant, provision must always be made for the individual examination of those children who require to be furnished with labour passes.*

Exception schedules.

With regard to the exception schedules, the Report says that while the teachers are unanimous in their complaints that the inspectors look unfavourably on withdrawals, managers, on the other hand, do not share that

---

* Mr. Alderson dissents from the proposal to extend compulsory recorded individual examination from children qualified by attendance to all children attending the school, and thinks that the examination should be by classes, and that the report of the inspector should summarize the attainments of the children in the several classes.

opinion, and the inspectors as a whole speak in defence of the existing system, maintaining that they deal fairly with the exception schedule, and do not refuse exceptions in those cases where sufficient reasons are given.

Having made special inquiry into the existence and **Over-** causes of over-pressure among the teachers and scholars **pressure.** in elementary schools, the Commission find considerable difference of opinion existing, although inspectors are on the whole unanimous in thinking that there is very little over-pressure. The Commission consider that many children attending school are not fit for study, which is attributable in many cases to their being insufficiently fed, and to the fact that many sickly children necessarily attend school who must inevitably be affected by any over-strain. Further, they say there is no doubt but that the present system of "payment by results," although an exaggerated evil, tends in some degree to produce over-pressure. As a result of the statistical inquiries made by the Commission, it appears that about 30 per cent. of voluntary managers, school boards, and head teachers allege some kind of over-pressure. The Commission think that better feeding, the employment of larger and more efficient teaching staffs, together with a better distribution of work and improved attendance would do much to mitigate this evil. It is regarded as of special importance that great care should be taken to secure pupil-teachers for apprenticeship who are constitutionally strong and healthy. With regard to over-pressure as a result of the present system of payment the Commission are of opinion that—

" So long as a money value is attached to each success in the
" individual examination of the children attending any ele-
" mentary school, and so long as the teachers are dependent on
" the grant for part of their income, there is great risk that

"teachers in considering their own reputation and emolu-
"ments may endanger the health and welfare of the children.
"We give due weight to Mr. Fitch's explanation of the reason
"why the outcry against this evil broke out when it did—
"namely, that whereas before the Code of 1882 it was to the
"interest of the teacher to present as many children as
"possible for examination, under that Code it became his
"interest to withdraw all who were unlikely to pass success-
"fully. But we cannot forget that we have to deal with
"circumstances as they exist, and with human nature as we
"find it; we are unable, therefore, to look for a complete
"remedy for over-pressure without some modification of the
"regulations of the existing Code."

Recommen-
dations as
to future
Inspections.　　　As to future inspections the following recommendations
are made, viz., that there should be two distinct inspections
held on different days within a fortnight of each other;
that the first should consist of a thorough individual
examination in the three elementary subjects, the
results of which should be designated "the report of
the examination;" this report to be placed in the hands of
the inspector of the district, who should himself make the
second examination by any methods he may select, for the
purpose of passing judgment upon the whole character
of the school, giving advice and encouragement to
managers and teachers, and testing the general proficiency
of the children in all the subjects taught; the inspector's
report on the school to be based upon the results of both
inspections.* It is further recommended that the inspector
should, if he thinks it desirable, test the report of the first
examination, and that an appeal should rest from his final
judgment to the chief inspector of the division.

* Mr. Alderson would have preferred that no rigid rule were laid down on
the subject. He thinks this recommendation will involve administrative
difficulties in apportioning the work between inspector and assistant, and will
discourage visits without notice, to which he attaches great value.

CHAPTER XIV.

PARLIAMENTARY GRANT.

HAVING briefly reviewed the regulations governing the **Code of 1862.** distribution of the Parliamentary grant both before and after the introduction of Mr. Lowe's Revised Code of 1862, since which grants have been paid to schools according to the results of individual examination, the Commission proceed to consider the effects of this system, popularly known as " payment by results."

The evidence given by teachers upon this subject **Payment by** is regarded by the Commission as a very heavy indictment **results.** against the system, on the ground that money payments for particular subjects discourage all intellectual teaching, and offer an incentive to teachers simply to work from mercenary motives. Thus, it is alleged, " Cramming " and " Over-pressure " are the natural results.

Some managers are distinctly in favour of retaining the present system, amongst them being Mr. Diggle and Mr. Birley, seeing in it the only true guarantee to the State that the education given in aided schools is efficient, and that every child shares in it.

On the other hand others condemn it as strongly as the teachers, notably Sir Lovelace Stamer, Dr. Crosskey, Mr. Wilks, and Mr. MacCarthy, characterising it as only a partial guarantee to the State of the child's learning, and that teachers are made to think how they can get children through the examination rather than of their advancement in education. The Commission, however, are of opinion that the uprightness and zeal of the teachers have largely mitigated any evils that may have arisen under the present system, notwithstanding the temptations to which they have been exposed.

Knowledge imparted soon lost. The evidence given by various witnesses to the effect that children after leaving school quickly lose the knowledge imparted to them, leads the Commission to think that the bad effects of a system of "cram" are on the increase, and that a great change is necessary to diminish this evil.

Conclusion. But after weighing carefully all the evidence, they are unable to propose that the grant should be wholly disconnected from its present dependence on the results of individual examination, since they are convinced that there would be a risk of incurring greater evils. Nevertheless they are unanimously agreed that the system of "payment by results" is carried too far, is too rigidly applied, and ought to be relaxed in the interests of education.

Distribution of grant. A table is given in the Report setting out the different heads under which the grant is at present distributed, which shows that more than two-thirds of the whole is variable and uncertain; so that managers of voluntary schools are always left in some suspense as to the amount that will be available for the support of their schools.*

Fixed and variable grants. Before making their own recommendations the Commission mention the remedies suggested by various witnesses. It is asserted that teachers and managers were practically unanimous, while the inspectors were divided on the point, that the fixed grant which depends on attendance should be increased, and that dependent on the results of examination proportionally diminished. Some witnesses proposed the re-adjustment of the items of the variable grant, others the abolition of the variable

* See note at end of chapter (page 80).

grant, making the whole grant one of general merit; others would substitute class examination for individual examination; and others again would abolish the merit grant altogether. With regard to this grant, which was first introduced in the Code of 1882, in order to encourage a higher quality of education and to discourage mere mechanical results, the Commission, after referring to the evidence before them, which on the whole goes to show that the object of this grant has not been wholly fulfilled, express their opinion that the instructions to inspectors seem to have thrown upon it a burden considerably in excess of the letter of the Code, and much beyond what the small amount of the grant can properly bear. It appears also, they say, that in assessing it the "special circumstances" of individual schools have not been sufficiently taken into account.

Merit grant.

The Commission, however, admitting the drawbacks and difficulties involved in assessing the merit grant, say that if the plan of the distribution of the grant, which they hereinafter recommend, be not adopted, the weight of evidence is against the retention of the merit grant in its present form in schools for older children. Accordingly they make the following suggestion :—

Recommen- dations.

"That the classification of schools as 'Fair,' 'Good,' or
" 'Excellent,' be discontinued. .   .   .   .   .
" We suggest that if the present system of payment by results
" be retained, it would be better that the moneys now avail-
" able for the merit grant be devoted in such proportions
" as the inspector may deem expedient to reward superior
" intelligence displayed by scholars in particular subjects,
" and other merits also not now recognized by grants, the
" particular merits for which these grants are awarded by
" the inspector being stated in his report. Organization
" and methods of instruction are best left free from the con-

" trol of the inspector, who may certainly advise respecting
" them, but should not, in our opinion, have it in his power
" either to fine or to pay the school directly for them as
" items in the grant. If he does so, there is danger lest an
" unwise passion for uniformity should lead either the
" inspector or the Education Department unduly to interfere
" with the different methods of school management and
" instruction which may be taught in our training colleges,
" or which are being tried by different school managers and
" teachers."

17s. 6d. limit.

Against the 17s. 6d. limit there is almost an universal
objection, the chief grounds of complaint being that
it presses hardly upon small and poor schools, that by
it teachers and managers are discouraged in their efforts
to improve their schools, and that it is contrary to a
professed principle of the Code, viz., "payment by
results." Some managers and inspectors would abolish it
altogether, others desire that it should be raised. Lord
Lingen contended for the imposition of a double limit, one
to prevent the grant ever exceeding the locally raised
income, and the other to keep the whole grant below a
fixed sum to be determined by the district and by a scale
specially adjusted thereto.

Conclusion.

Taking all the evidence into consideration the Commission express their conclusion in the following terms:—

" In weighing all the evidence for and against the 17s. 6d. limit,
" we are compelled to admit that it acts as a discouragement
" to improvement in certain cases, and we recommend
" that the provision in the Elementary Education Act of
" 1876, upon which this limitation is based be accordingly
" repealed. We see, however, some danger in the proposal
" to abolish all limits, for we have little doubt that, in many
" instances, school managers now make efforts to keep up
" the amount of the local income of their school, in order

" not to lose any part of the grant earned, efforts which
" they would be tempted to relax if restriction were
" wholly swept away. Nor do we think that the amount of
" the Parliamentary grant per head will bear indefinite
" expansion. We think, therefore, that any modification of
" the present limits must be considered in relation to the
" general question of the total amount of the Parliamentary
" grant."

As the education in sparsely populated districts has *Special grants to small schools.* since 1876 been provided for by Parliament by special grant, the Commission recommend that this aid might be still further increased, and that all schools having an average attendance of not less than 100, not being within two miles of any other available school, or difficult of access, should receive a special grant increasing by 6s. 8d. for each child less than 100 in average attendance, a maximum grant of £20 being payable to schools with not more than 40 in average attendance. This special grant is regarded as one that will facilitate the enforcement of the extended curriculum recommended as the minimum, and as providing for the additional cost of maintaining an increased staff of teachers.

The Commission also recommend that this grant *Expenditure should be limited.* should only be given to those schools where the fees are, in the opinion of the Department, sufficiently low to render them available for the poorest inhabitants of these districts, and that it should not be affected by any general rule as to the reduction of the grant.

Whilst on this subject, the attention of the Commission *Economical limits.* was drawn to the evidence of certain witnesses, from whose statements it appears that economical considerations were apparently disregarded; and in view of the fact that the standard of examination, and consequently the expenditure, have risen largely since the Act of 1870, they consider that some limit ought to be placed on the cost of the maintenance of aided schools, due regard being paid to their efficiency without undue strain on local resources.

It is, however, regarded as impossible to place any maximum limit on the expenditure adapted to meet the varying circumstances of public elementary schools, and it is thought that reasons exist for hoping that where, in the case of some school boards, there has hitherto been extravagance, the vigilance of the ratepayers will bring about a diminished expenditure.

Recommendations as to the future distribution of the grant. The Commission are of opinion that in some form each of the three constituent elements of the variable grant should be retained. They recommend that the fixed grant should be increased to 10s. per child in average attendance, and that the conditions of the fluctuating grants should be so modified as to depend upon the good character of the school and the quality of the acquirements of the great majority of the scholars.*

In order to increase the efficiency of schools in the future, and at the same time to diminish the over-anxiety of managers, teachers, and children, it is proposed that the average amount of the variable grant in present circumstances should be not less than 10s. per scholar.

To carry out these recommendations the Commission think it would be necessary to treat the individual examination as a means for merely testing the general

---

* Lord Norton would wish to see the present mode of Parliamentary support, by payments on piece-work in detail, entirely abandoned, and would have instead fixed and adequate support for each school; all doubt, he says, as to whether this simpler mode, pursued by all other nations, is applicable here, being removed by the fact that some of the larger school boards have already adopted it.

progress of the scholars, and not for the purpose of assessing individual grants.

As a child's future improvement depends so much on an intelligent knowledge of the elementary subjects, it is further thought that special stress should be laid upon efficiency in reading, writing, and arithmetic in distributing the variable grant.

The inspector's report of the school, it is suggested, should include each of the following points: (1) Moral training; (2) Cleanliness, both of school and scholars; (3) Quietness; (4) Attention; (5) Obedience; (6) Accuracy of knowledge; (7) General intelligence; (8) Classification; (9) Instruction of pupil-teachers; and should record in detail the results of examination in each subject, stating specifically the grounds on which any reduction of grant is recommended.

In addition to these important alterations, the Commission say they regard it as necessary that where the incompetence of a teacher has been proved, and due notice has been given, the Department should have power to declare the school in default, and to suspend payment of the grant, and to make deductions in the grant for any grave faults in the conduct or management of a school Another suggestion offered is that a part of the Parliamentary grant might be employed in paying a portion of the salary of organizing masters, or local inspectors, or even in contributing towards the expense of itinerant teachers of science and drawing.

The Commission recommend that the managers of a school which has been passed as "efficient" and "suitable," on being ordered, under pain of default, by the Department, to make alterations in the premises, should receive a grant in aid of the work from the State.

They further express the opinion that the different methods of school management or teaching should be left free from the control of the inspector, and that managers should be placed beyond the caprice of the Ministry of the day with respect to the Parliamentary grant in whatever form it is given. They also think that the terms upon which the grant is to be awarded should be embodied in an Act of Parliament, and not be as hitherto left dependent on a Minute of the Privy Council.

It is also recommended that when any changes have to be made, a copy of the Code containing them should be laid before Parliament in print at least two months before coming into force.

NOTE (see page 74).—The following grants are now obtainable in boys', girls', and infants' schools :—

Boys' and Girls' Schools.

	s.	d.	
1. Fixed grant on the *average attendance* ..	4	6	per head.
2. Merit grant, fair	1	0	,,
,, good	2	0	,,
,, excellent	3	0	,,
3. Singing by ear	0	6	,,
,, note.. ′	1	0	,,
4. Needlework (girls)	1	0	,,
5. On examination in the three elementary subjects (maximum)..	8	4	,,
6. Class subjects, of which two ⎱ Fair	1	0	,,
may be taken .. ⎰ Good ..	2	0	,,
7. Specific subjects for each pass in not more than two subjects	2	0	,,
8. Cookery, for each girl in Standard IV and upwards who has received the prescribed instruction	4	0	,,

Infants' Schools.

	s.	d.
1. Fixed grant	9	0
2. Merit ,, ...	6	0
3. Needlework	1	0
4. Singing	1	0

It appears therefore from the foregoing list of grants, that the highest amount attainable under the present system, without specific subjects and cookery, is :—

	£	s.	d.
In boys' schools	1	0	10
„ girls' „	1	1	10
„ infants' „	0	17	0

For girls, however, in Standards IV and upwards, a further grant of 4s. per head may be earned for practical cookery; and in Standards V and upwards an additional sum of 2s. for each of not more than two specific subjects in the case of boys, and of one specific subject in the case of girls who take up cookery, making the maximum grant attainable for children in the higher standards to be :—

	£	s.	d.
Boys (Standards V—VII)	1	4	10
Girls (Standard IV)	1	5	10
„ (Standards V—VII)	1	7	10

CHAPTER XV.

INCOME AND EXPENDITURE OF SCHOOLS.

THE Commission make some preliminary remarks upon the growing cost of elementary education, the average annual cost per scholar in average attendance during the past twelve years having risen from £1 14s. 8d. to £1 19s. 5d. This increase of expenditure is attributed in part to the higher salaries now paid to the teachers. *Increased cost of elementary education and its causes.*

The Report quotes the opinion of Lord Lingen that the cost per scholar is unnecessarily large, which he attributed partly to a rise in the teachers' salaries, while an increased Parliamentary grant had led to extravagance, the increased expenditure being largely due to the rivalry between board and voluntary schools.

As to the sources of the fund for elementary education —viz., the Parliamentary grant, local resources (rates or subscriptions), endowments, and school fees—attention is drawn in the Report to the rapid increase in the amount *The burden on the central Government.*

G

of grant per head, which has risen from 10s. 6d. in 1860 to 17s. 2½d. in 1886, the total grant amounting to £2,866,700 out of a total income of £6,827,189. Lord Lingen considers this the natural result of the Act of 1876, and advocates the reduction of the Parliamentary grant to one-third of the whole cost.

Lord Lingen's scheme. With regard to Lord Lingen's plan for carrying this proposal into effect, the Report says:—

> " He would sweep away the present complicated system, for
> " he considered that it exposes the State to 'demands on a
> " variety of points, on some of which, from time to time,
> " demands for more money are made with success,' and that
> " it 'has a tendency to increase the aid that is to be obtained
> " from the State, as being the subscriber on whom, through
> " a great variety of accesses, the greatest pressure can be
> " exercised.' In its stead he would bring in a system pro-
> " viding that the State should give a fixed subsidy, bearing a
> " certain fair proportion to the whole cost of education, that
> " that subsidy should be paid to and distributed by local
> " bodies, hereafter to be created, with considerable areas of
> " administration, and having ample powers to raise other
> " money by local rates, and that these local bodies should
> " be empowered to propose equitable and liberal terms
> " to the denominational schools, so as to induce them to
> " co-operate in the new scheme."

The burden on the rates. With regard to that part of the cost of education which is borne by the rates, the Commission point out that although the Education Department returns for 1886 show that £1,279,916 was raised for school maintenance from rates in England and Wales, the other charges upon the education rate raised the sum total to £2,526,495. This amount, it is said, would be very largely increased but for the existence of voluntary schools, the transfer of whose scholars to School Boards would involve an additional cost to the rates of £2,000,000 a year, besides a large outlay for building schools in place of those not transferred to school boards.

It is reported that the voluntary subscriptions have increased from £418,839 in 1870 to £732,524 in 1884. Much complaint is made by the supporters of voluntary schools that they not only provide voluntary contributions, but also have to pay school board rates. The suggestions made to the Commission for their relief were twofold, first, that voluntary schools should share in the rates; secondly, that the rates of voluntary subscribers should be reduced by the amount of their subscriptions to a voluntary school. *The burden on voluntary subscribers.*

Lord Lingen in his evidence laid stress upon the fact that as voluntary schools do not share in the rates, it is much more difficult for them to exist than it is for board schools, and he would therefore propose to put them on a financial equality by giving to each a share of the rates. *Lord Lingen's plan.*

" Supposing," he says, " you had the whole country mapped
" out under educational authorities, I should then like the
" State to deal only with those local authorities and to pay
" them a certain proportion which, I think, might be calcu-
" lated on the population. I then would take away the bar
" which the 14th section " (the Cowper-Temple clause of the
" Act of 1870) " now imposes upon aiding those schools
" which adopt precise religious instruction. That bar I
" would take away. Inasmuch as the local bodies would
" have to tax themselves for the work done by the voluntary
" schools if they failed, my impression is, that if left to
" themselves they would come to terms with the voluntary
" schools."

Lord Lingen is of opinion that the independence of the voluntary schools in the selection of teachers, and in re-spect to the religious and moral discipline, "would be absolutely uninterfered with."

" Under this plan the local authority," he says, "would have
" to work the detailed examination of the schools; and the
" central authority would have to work the general inspec-
" tion of the schools."

The Commission however regard the difficulties in
any attempt to repeal the Cowper-Temple clause as too
great for them to recommend the acceptance of this plan
by Parliament on condition of such repeal.

But Lord Lingen is not understood by the Commission
to favour the total abolition of the Cowper-Temple clause;
and since voluntary schools are not necessarily affected by
it, inasmuch as they now receive aid from the rates in
the form of fees from the guardians for poor children, the
Commission think the principle might be extended, and
that rate-aid for secular efficiency might be given to
voluntary schools, unaffected by any such clause as that
contained in the Act of 1870. It is also recognized that
voluntary schools have a claim to public resources, first
because the long purse which the board schools are able to
draw upon involves the voluntary schools in increased
expenditure, and secondly since both systems equally
form part of the machinery of national education, voluntary subscribers save their respective localities from
many heavy burdens. The Commission think that the
time has come for a new departure, since the country is
now provided with a national system of education; and
that if education, as one of the most important branches
of the new local government scheme, could gradually be
connected with the civil administration of each locality,
much of the existing unhealthy rivalry between the two
systems of voluntary and board schools would be
diminished, and the consequent expenditure reduced.
It is also thought that the Education Department would

thereby be relieved of much unnecessary routine work, whilst fully retaining its valuable powers of general control.

So long as managers subscribe towards the cost of voluntary schools, it is recognized by the Report as only reasonable that they should retain their management of them; but it does not seem just to the Commission that the board schools, with their unlimited resources, should be allowed gradually to destroy the voluntary system. Accordingly it is recommended :— **Voluntary schools to be assisted out of the rates.**

" That the local educational authority be empowered to sup- **Conclusion.**
" plement from local rates the voluntary subscriptions given
" to the support of every public State-aided elementary school
" in their district, to an amount equal to these subscriptions,
" provided it does not exceed the amount of ten shillings for
" each child in average attendance. Where a school attend-
" ance committee is the authority, the rate should be
" chargeable to the separate school district affected. The **Prospective**
" school boards might in time, if not at once, be merged in **legislation.**
" the local authorities charged with the general civil admin-
" istration. Every voluntary school might in that case
" receive some return from the rates to which its supporters
" contributed ; while every ratepayer would be interested in
" the welfare of the schools of this class, because he would
" know that the rates would be increased by the burden of
" supplying the place, out of the rates, of such of these
" schools as might cease to form part of the efficient supply
" of the district."*

* Archdeacon Smith dissents from the recommendation to give voluntary schools a share in the local rates on the following grounds :—

(i.) That the settlement of 1870 would be thereby re-opened.

(ii.) That it would involve the repeal of the Cowper-Temple clause.

(iii.) That it would give the ratepayers a right to share in the management, which would not be to the advantage of voluntary schools.

(iv.) That it would involve the levy of a substantial school rate in parishes where there is no School Board.

(v.) That it would involve an unnecessary expenditure of public money without any corresponding advantage.

The rating of schools. Another complaint made by managers of voluntary schools is, that they have to pay rates upon their buildings towards the maintenance of board schools, and also that whilst the whole body of ratepayers have to pay the rates out of which the board schools are supported, the voluntary contributors exclusively have to provide the money for their schools. The general feeling of a large proportion of the witnesses is against the continued assessment to the rates of public elementary schools, special reference being made to Mr. Diggle's opinion, that "the incidence of it is unjust and inequitable." The Commission accordingly recommend that public elementary schools for which no rent is paid or received should be exempt from local rates.

Remission of school fees. Passing on to consider the methods in vogue for paying the fees of pauper children, which take the form in the case of board schools of the power to remit fees, and in the case of voluntary schools, of the payment of fees by the guardians, several objections to this latter method are mentioned, such as the difficulty of obtaining the payment of fees by the guardians, and the humiliation which parents feel in being often compelled to apply *in formâ pauperis*.

Conclusions. After referring to the various suggestions made for mitigating this grievance, the Commission say that it would be highly desirable that applications for the payment of school fees should be entertained by boards of guardians quite apart from claims for out-door relief, and that inquiries should be instituted into the circumstances of applicants, instead of requiring their personal attendance.

They are also of opinion that in all cases the guardians should pay fees direct to the managers, and that they should be required to pay fees for the children under five of indigent parents, or for those children who have passed the limit of obligatory school attendance, where parents are willing to send them to school. In the event of district councils being established by the new Local Government Bill, it is recommended that the payment of the fees of indigent children should be entrusted to them, and charged upon the rates; and further, that the councils should have the power of appointing local committees in each parish, before whom the applications for the payment of school fees might be heard.

The Commission cannot recommend that the regulation of fees in voluntary schools should be entrusted to the Education Department, an effectual remedy, they point out, already existing against excessive fees, since the Inspector of the district can report a school to the Department where the fees are too high for the population, as unsuitable to form part of the school accommodation of the district. *The censorship of fees by the Department.*

Reference is made to the evidence of several witnesses who advocated the total abolition of school fees, their chief contentions being: 1. That it is a corollary of the system of compulsion. 2. That the fee system hinders education, since the parents continually urge poverty as an excuse for keeping their children at home. 3. That the abolition of fees would promote regularity of attendance. 4. That the collection of fees is a waste of time to the teachers, and the whole system a cause of worry. 5. That the fees bear very heavily on the poor man. *Free Education, what the advocates say.*

On the other hand those who are opposed to free education, say: 1. That parents are not oppressed by the fees, since when they are out of work their children are often allowed to attend school without the fee. 2. That *What the opponents say.*

free education is not demanded by the parents. 3. That
the payment of school fees favours regularity, since
parents like to have full measure for their money. 4. That
those schools appear to be the most popular where the
highest fees are charged. 5. That parents take a pride
in paying for their children's education. 6. That with the
abolition of fees those who have no children to educate
would complain of having to pay as much by way of rates
as the parents of children attending the schools.

Opinion of the Commission. The Commission conclude their reference to the
question of free education with the following expression
of opinion :—

> " If, as we think, provision of the due necessaries of education,
> " as well as of the necessaries of life, is part of the responsi-
> " bility incumbent on parents, it may well be believed that
> " public contributions and private benevolence are already
> " doing all that can be safely required of them in augmenta-
> " tion of the payments properly exacted from parents. On the
> " whole, we are of opinion that the balance of advantage is
> " greatly in favour of maintaining the present system, estab-
> " lished by the Act of 1870, whereby the parents who can
> " afford it contribute a substantial proportion of the cost of
> " the education of their children in the form of school fees."

CHAPTER XVI.

LOCAL EDUCATIONAL AUTHORITIES.

Election of School Boards. IN considering the two classes of local educational authority,
namely, the School Board and the School Attendance
Committee, the first question raised is the method of
the election of school boards as defined by section 29

of the Act of 1870,* which enables even small minorities of the electors to be represented on the Board. With regard to this system, known as the cumulative vote, Lord Lingen and Mr. Cumin are substantially in agreement in wishing to retain the cumulative vote, on the ground that it secures the election of a more responsible and representative body of managers. The cumulative vote.

On the other hand, several witnesses spoke of the anomalies and inconvenience resulting from the cumulative vote, such as the defeat of desirable candidates, and the election of representatives on other than educational grounds. The Commission, while recognizing the drawbacks of cumulative voting, are on the whole in favour of retaining some form of proportional representation in School Board elections, and recommend the adoption of the single transferable vote, which possesses the advantages without the inconvenience of the cumulative vote. Conclusion.

In explanation of this recommendation the Report says, " In the system known as the single transferable vote, under which the elector places the number 1, 2, 3 against the several candidates in the order of his preference, the surplus votes of any candidate are passed over to another in the manner indicated by the elector. This obviates the waste of voting power, diminishes the opportunity of wire-pulling, and is simpler than the present system." The further opinion is expressed that it would be advisable to divide the larger towns into constituencies, returning not more than five members each.

The next point discussed is the expense attending Expense of elections.

---

* Section XXIX, Act of 1870, provides that at every School Board election every voter shall be entitled to a number of votes equal to the number of the members of the School Board to be elected, and may give all such votes to one candidate, or may distribute them among the candidates as he thinks fit.

candidature at School Board elections, which according to several witnesses is said to be not only a serious inconvenience to candidates, but also an injury to the cause of education, instances having occurred where such elections had cost single candidates as much as £700, and in one case even more than £1,000. The Commission however think that their previous recommendation will have the effect of diminishing the great expense of elections.

Interference in elections.

Mention is made of one abuse which came under notice, viz., the interference of board school teachers in elections, and the Commission are of opinion that School Boards ought to use their power in putting an end to such a practice.

Period for which Boards should be elected.

With regard to the length of time for which boards should be elected, the prevalent opinion appears to be that the term of office should be lengthened, to meet the complaints that the present triennial elections prevent a continuity of policy. The Commission however are not prepared to make any recommendations pending legislative changes with regard to local government, although they think that a somewhat longer term of office with partial renewal would be an improvement on the present method.

Universal School Boards.

A good deal of evidence both for and against the universal establishment of School Boards was given before the Commission, who think that much of the existing strong feeling of dislike to School Boards is due not so much to jealousy or dread of interference on the part of representative ratepayers in the work of school management, as to disapproval of the restriction of distinctive religious teaching imposed upon rate-supported schools by the Act of 1870.

School

Some difficulty is encountered in drawing a conclusion

as to the efficient working of the local authorities, owing to **Attendance Com-** the fact that the results of the working of compulsion **mittees.** are so dependent on a variety of causes; but on the whole the Commission are of opinion that School Attendance Committees in rural districts have administered compulsion at least as well as the rural School Boards.

It is recommended that an annual return be made to **Recom-** the Education Department by School Attendance Commit- **mendation.** tees, rendering a full account of their work, and any information relative to their duties which is required of them, thus affording the Department a better opportunity of dealing with any obvious shortcomings.

Mention is here made of a proposal to group together **Grouping** small rural School Boards so as to represent a larger area **of small School** than at present, the Union being suggested as the only **Board** legally recognized area offering itself for such a purpose. **areas.** The Commission, however, in the present uncertainty as to the form which county government may take, make no definite recommendations as to the future nature and powers of local educational authorities.*

* Cardinal Manning, in signing the Report, remarks that it has not treated of the one subject which he believes to be chief in importance, namely, the unjust inequality in the position of the voluntary system in relation to the new system of school boards. It has hitherto, His Eminence says, appeared very improbable that the Commission should close its Report without pointing out these unjust inequalities and without suggesting at least in outline some future legislative remedy.

REPORT OF THE "MINORITY."

CHAPTER I.

POINTS OF AGREEMENT WITH THE "MAJORITY."

THE "Minority" of the Commission, after expressing their regret that they were unable to sign the Report of the "Majority," point out the following important conclusions of that Report to which they give their assent, in order that these matters may have the benefit of the combined support of the whole Commission :—

School Supply.

They agree—

1. That accommodation is needed throughout England and Wales for one-sixth of the population; though in certain districts the requirements amount to nearly a fifth.

Structural Suitability of School Supply.

2. Very generally with the opinions and recommendations as to the structural suitability of the present school supply as set out in the chapter of the Report of the "Majority."

School Management.

3. That the "farming" of schools to teachers should be prevented.

4. That the accounts of voluntary schools should be made public.

5. That co-operation among managers of voluntary schools would greatly improve these schools, and that they would be glad to see help given towards the salaries of inspectors, science teachers, &c.

H.M. Inspectors.

6. Generally, in the recommendations as to inspectors, laying special stress on opening all ranks of the inspectorate to elementary teachers, and on the importance of the previous practical experience of inspectors as teachers.

Teachers and Staff.

7. That the teachers ought to be paid fixed salaries.

8. That it is desirable that the head teacher should not be dissociated from actual instruction in addition to general superintendence; but that no definite rule should be made interfering with the discretion of managers and head teachers in the organization of the school.

9. That the imperfect preparation of students at entrance is a serious obstacle to their progress in training colleges.

10. That the Code requirements as to staff should be considerably increased.

11. That pupil-teachers, especially those in their first year of service, should be allowed more time during school hours for their studies than is now common, and that the instruction given by the head teachers should be, wherever possible, supplemented in respect of some of the compulsory, as well as the optional subjects, by central class teaching.

12. That extra grants should be offered to those managers who successfully adopt this course.

13. That where central class teaching is obviously impossible, grants should be made to managers who successfully employ other special means to secure the thorough instruction of their pupil-teachers.

Training Colleges.

14. That, while regretting the limitations which restrict the force of the recommendations of their colleagues, a third year of training should be allowed for a certain number of selected students, and the extension of training generally, by the association of day students with places of higher general education, and that a conscience clause for day students, who might be admitted to the existing training colleges, should be introduced.

Attendance and Compulsion.

15. That the minimum age for half-time exemption should be 11, and for full-time 13, and that half-time should

only be conceded to those who are "beneficially and necessarily" employed at work.

16. That the process of recovering fines under the Summary Jurisdiction Act of 1879 by distress instead of by commitment has, in some cases, encouraged parents to defy the law, and has added greatly to the labour involved in carrying out compulsion.

17. That truant schools should be established; and local committees more generally appointed under the Act of 1876, Section 32, and that school attendance committees should hold meetings from time to time in various parts of their districts.

18. That theatrical employment should be brought under the Factory Acts, with necessary modifications.

Curriculum.

19. That drawing should, as far as practicable, be a compulsory subject for all boys, and under suitable conditions encouraged in the case of girls.

20. That history might be introduced earlier than at present; that the practical teaching of cookery should be extended, and that the present special preference of English above the other class subjects should be removed from the Code.

21. That teaching singing by ear should continue to be recognized, but they believe that gradually singing by note may become practically universal; that systematized physical exercises should be extended, and that it is through the training colleges that a safe and scientific system should be introduced by making instruction in these exercises and some knowledge of physiology, a point of the school curriculum.

22. In the minimum curriculum laid down for village schools.

23. In recommending an increase in the number of reading books, the diminution of the importance to be attached to spelling, especially in the lower standards, the reconstruction of the arithmetic standards, and the importance of securing an intelligent understanding of arithmetical principles as well as mechanical accuracy in the application of rules.

Various Classes of Elementary Schools.

24. In recommending several schemes of instruction, so as to provide for various classes of schools curricula

varying in breadth and completeness with the number of scholars in attendance, and with the character and requirements of the population, although regret is expressed that no additional aid is recommended towards the increased cost of such an extended scheme.

25. In the establishment of school libraries in every school, and the inexpediency of introducing recognized Government text-books.

26. They agree heartily with the very valuable recommendations as to evening schools, and generally with their colleagues on industrial and workhouse schools.

27. They agree generally on the recommendations as to Welsh schools.

Higher Elementary Schools.

They also agree—

28. That higher Elementary Schools are a useful, (they add a necessary), addition to school machinery for primary education, and that due precautions should be taken not to exclude the promising children of poor parents from the privileges to be enjoyed in them.

29. That, where these schools cannot be founded, higher classes for children who have passed Standard VII should be attached to an ordinary elementary school, and that the supply of satisfactory secondary schools should be organized and made adequate for the wants of all parts of the country, and that increased funds should be provided out of which to create sufficient exhibitions for deserving elementary scholars needing further instruction at these schools.

Income and Expenditure.

30. That facilities should be given whereby poor persons may obtain the payment of moderate school fees for their children in voluntary as well as in board schools, without any association with ideas of pauperism, and that the guardians should pay the fees of the children of those receiving out-door relief direct to school managers.

31. That fees should be paid for the children of poor persons, whether such children are under five years old or exempt from legal obligation to attend school.

Local Educational Authorities.

32. That in the event of some form of proportional representation being retained (as to which the "Minority"

are not unanimous), large towns should be divided into constituencies returning not more than five members each, a majority of the dissentients thinking that they should be elected by the single transferable vote.

33. That a longer term of office, with partial renewal, would be an improvement in the constitution of School Boards.

Mr. Heller agrees with the Commission with regard to their scheme of retiring pensions (see page 22), but thinks the maximum augmentation of £15 too low, and that Article 13½ of the Code should include all who were pupil teachers before August, 1862.

Note.—This chapter has been signed by the following : The Hon. E. Lyulph Stanley, Sir John Lubbock, Bart., M.P., Sir Bernhard Samuelson, Bart., M.P., Dr. R. W. Dale, Mr. Sydney Buxton, M.P., Mr. H. Richard, M.P., Mr. T. E. Heller, and Mr. G. Shipton. The conclusions and recommendations contained in the remaining chapters are agreed to only by the following five, Hon. E. Lyulph Stanley, Dr. R. W. Dale, Mr. H. Richard, M.P., Mr. T. E. Heller, and Mr. G. Shipton, except where otherwise it is specially stated.

CHAPTER II.

SCHOOL SUPPLY.

Basis for calculating school supply. HAVING examined the supply and the position of efficient schools since the passing of the Act of 1870, the "Minority" (agreeing with the "Majority") express their opinion that the estimate of one-sixth of the population, for whom school provision has been considered hitherto by the Department to be necessary, is a moderate one, and that in districts where the individual population is large, one-fifth corresponds more nearly with the needs of the locality. But assuming that all the places in the public elementary schools of the country are available and suitable, which is not admitted by them, it is thought that the deficiencies of school accommodation would have been substantially overtaken.

Provision for infants. As to the provision for children between the ages of 3 and 13, although there was a witness before the Commission who urged that infants should not be reckoned in estimating the school population, the "Minority" say that there was an overwhelming mass of testimony in favour of retaining them, and although no opinion is expressed as to the exact proportion for which the supply for infants should be provided, they think the accommodation should be ample, and the attendance of those under 5 years of age encouraged.*

With regard to the demand for new schools, which, it **Right of** is said, still continues in urban and populous districts, and **School** can only be effectually met by the action of School Boards, **Boards to** the "Minority" assert that the practice of the Department **schools.** has put administrative hindrances in the way of exercising that power of providing schools which was clearly conferred on School Boards by Section 18 of the Act, 1870. (See note page 3.) It is said that the School Board was already intended to have power at its own discretion to set up schools if it could dispense with the aid of the Department in the building of the schools, but that the Department claims the power by withholding its consent to the fee to be charged in a school, both preventing it from being conducted as a public elementary school in compliance with the Code, and subjecting the Board to a surcharge.

Whilst it is necessary, the "Minority" say, that the Department should have all the powers given by the Act to compel School Boards to build efficient schools, it is of no advantage to education to prevent a School Board from establishing a school where they think one necessary.

The opinion is expressed that buildings dedicated to the **Transfer of** purpose of elementary education, and aided by a building **a school to** grant, should, if the existing managers are unable or un- **a School** willing to conduct schools in them, be transferred to the **Board.** local authority charged with the duty of making sufficient school provision for the district; and also that any building aided by a building grant, not used on week-days for the education of the poor, if it existed for that purpose, should be used by the School Board for supplying school accommodation for their district.

For the contention that the Education Act of 1870 **Application** was intended for the working class only, and that it is **of the Act** an abuse for the public elementary schools to be used **not limited.** by well-to-do children, the "Minority" say that such an opinion finds no support in, and is inconsistent with, the Act, which imposed only one restriction as to fees, namely, that the ordinary payments should not exceed 9d. per scholar. This fact, it is pointed out, is an important one to remember, because the only reason why schools are not demanded for all the population between

---

* On this point the "Minority" are unanimous in their opinion, though the "five" are further of opinion that any school building with a trust for elementary education should be treated in the same way.

certain ages is that many of the well-to-do abstain from
using the elementary schools, although they have a
perfect legal right to use them, and as the schools increase
in popularity and efficiency it is anticipated that those in
easy circumstances will use them more widely.

CHAPTER III.

STRUCTURAL SUITABILITY OF SCHOOL SUPPLY.

Accommo-
dation
requires
reviewing.
With regard to the suitability of the present school
supply, the "Minority" think that the time has come when
even in well-arranged schools 10 feet should be treated as
the minimum floor space for each child in average
attendance, and that this should apply to infant schools as
well as to senior departments.

Error of
reckoning
accommo-
dation.
The rule of measuring accommodation by the yearly
average attendance is said to be very mischievous in the
interests of school efficiency, it being contended that the
true measure should be the seat room required for those
on the roll, such supply to be authorized by the Department
according to the plans of the schools, and as it is shown
on the plans.

Lighting,
ventilation,
and
warming.
The lighting, ventilation, and warming of schools are
mentioned as very important matters in which there is
need for improvement, and the Department, it is recommended, should take more pains to secure this.

Play-
grounds.
Attention is drawn also to the value of playgrounds,
both morally and physically, and of the requirement by
the Department of the maximum area of site for all future
schools, namely, a quarter of an acre, though this is thought
to be an insufficient maximum.

School
equipment.
With regard to school furniture and premises, the
"Minority" say that much has been done by managers
towards improvement of late years, but that in rural
districts in some of the existing schools much is still needed
in this respect rather than the establishment of new schools.
They are of opinion that before any building is used as
a school, it should be approved, and the number of children
for whom it may be used certified by H.M. Inspector,

and that any building not so certified and used as a school should be closed. Further they think that in any proposed structural alterations, the interests of education alone should be considered, of which the Department is the proper guardian.*

The "Minority" have appended to this chapter a detailed examination of the case of Stockport, where the School Board was dissolved. They conclude from the figures given as to the dimensions of the school rooms, from the fees charged, and from other evidence, that the school supply is insufficient in quantity and bad in quality, that the fees are excessive, and the voluntary contributions inadequate, that the management is unfair, and that there is need for a School Board in that town.

The case of Stockport.

CHAPTER IV.

THE PUPIL-TEACHER SYSTEM.

(ON THE CONCLUSIONS IN THIS CHAPTER THE "MINORITY" ARE UNANIMOUSLY AGREED.)

AFTER tracing the history of the pupil-teacher system (which took its origin in the monitorial system of which it was a development and improvement), the "Minority" make reference to the opinion of Sir J. K. Shuttleworth, the author of the institution, that the pupil-teacher system was only intended to be transitional, and that adult teaching should gradually supersede it. The evidence before the Commission in reference to the pupil-teachers is regarded as very unfavourable, and that this is especially striking when given by those who are not prepared to see the system abolished.

Origin of the pupil-teacher system.

In discussing the question of the better instruction of pupil-teachers, the efforts which have been made in various parts of the country in order to remedy the defects under the present system are noticed, especially the central-class teaching as carried out by the Liverpool and London School Boards. The working of the centre system in Liverpool and London is given in detail, which shows

Central-class teaching.

* On this paragraph the "Minority" are unanimous in their opinion.

that it has been attended with marked success in comparison with the rest of England, and at a very small cost. The "Minority" say that the result of the work at the centres in London has been to secure a striking growth in the *esprit de corps* and sense of professional self-respect among the pupil-teachers, and that since the day centres have been at work, there has been a marked improvement in the quality of the candidates.

Recommendations. The "Minority" are agreed in thinking that pupil-teachers are a very unsatisfactory part of our school system, and, subject to their continuance, make the following recommendations with a view to their improvement :—

1. That no pupil-teachers should be permitted in a school where the head teacher is not specially certified by H.M. Inspector to take charge of them, and that no teacher should be so qualified until he has obtained his parchment.

2. That if, in the opinion of the inspector, the pupil-teachers have been neglected or badly trained by a head teacher, the inspector may recommend the disqualification of the head teacher for the charge of pupil-teachers.

3. That pupil-teachers should not during their first year at least be reckoned on the staff, and that unpromising pupil-teachers should have their engagement determined on the report of the inspector not later than the close of the third year.

4. That in country districts encouragement should be given to group pupil-teachers from neighbouring schools as far as possible for instruction.

5. That more time should be allowed them for study, and that less time should be spent in teaching in school, especially in the earlier years.

Results of the annual examination. With regard to the pupil-teachers' yearly examination, the "Minority" think that the results should be made known to the managers within a reasonable time of the end of the year, and that, if necessary, the matters not tested at the collective examination should be made the subject of a special visit to the school.

CHAPTER V.

EX-PUPIL-TEACHERS AND ACTING TEACHERS.

(ON THE CONCLUSIONS IN THIS CHAPTER THE "MINORITY"
ARE UNANIMOUSLY AGREED.)

THE "Minority" say that there is a great deal of testimony before the Commission to the effect that witnesses do not see how to dispense with pupil-teachers as a means of recruiting adult teachers, but that at the same time they are unsatisfactory as teachers, and ill-taught and ill-trained as scholars. This is attributed to the unprepared state in which the training colleges receive them, and although it is admitted that the training colleges do not always give a high quality of instruction, it is thought that if students on admission had been better taught, their education in college would be improved. *State of pupil-teachers on entering College.*

The oral evidence of several witnesses, and the replies of the Principals of Training Colleges to whom inquiries were addressed by the Commission, are quoted at some length, showing the unsatisfactory and uneducated state of candidates for admission to College, and the "Minority" are of opinion that the qualifications for candidates for training should be materially raised.

Passing on to consider the other kinds of adult teachers recognized, the "Minority" say that with regard to assistants under Article 84, they do not seem to have favourably impressed those who have seen them at work, and that if their services are to be continued, the least that can be required of them is that within a reasonable term (one year) they should qualify by passing, say, the scholarship examination. *Assistant-teachers under Article 84.*

As to ex-pupil-teachers, or assistant-teachers as they are designated by the Department, the testimony is regarded as very unfavourable to the annual examination as a satisfactory test, a failure to pass being practically unheard of, whilst about a quarter fail at the scholarship examination. *Ex-pupil-teachers.*

The following recommendations are made with regard to ex-pupil-teachers :— *Recommendations.*

1. That all ex-pupil-teachers should be required to sit for the scholarship examination in the July following the expiration of their apprenticeship, and pending the result of

the examination should only be recognized as assistants provisionally, and failing to pass high enough they should be disqualified at the ensuing Christmas from counting on the staff.

. 2. That ex-pupil-teachers should not be recognized beyond the age of 23 without passing the first year's examination for a certificate; and that having passed they should be required after an interval of not less than two years to pass the second year's certificate examination.

3. That ex-pupil-teachers should only be recognized as assistants.

Recommendations as to acting-teachers. As to acting-teachers the "Minority" are of opinion: 1. That, while the trained teachers are greatly superior to the untrained, it would not be wise to close all other avenues to the profession; 2. That the conditions of admission might be more stringent for untrained teachers; 3. That all acting teachers should be required to take the first year's papers not earlier than the Christmas year after they pass the scholarship examination, and the second year's papers not less than two years after passing the first year's examination; 4. That no acting teacher who has not obtained his parchment should be recognized as a head teacher, and that no person should be eligible for a head teachership who has not passed the second year's examination in a division not lower than the second.

CHAPTER VI.

TRAINING COLLEGES.

Future conditions of the Parliamentary grant for training. In this chapter the "Minority" deal with the assertion that any modification of the conditions on which the Parliamentary grant is in future to be given would be a breach of faith. (See page 26.) They reply that such a contention would convert the Parliamentary vote in effect to a charge on the Consolidated Fund, and that the claim to a vested interest in the grant without its being equitable for Parliament to modify its conditions comes too late in the day in this question of elementary education. To the further contention that the presence of those of different denominations in the same college is incompatible with college life, (see page 27,) the training colleges of the British and

Foreign School Society, the colleges of Oxford and Cambridge, Newnham, Girton, and Holloway colleges, where no difficulty arises, are pointed to as an answer. As a condition of continued State aid the "Minority" think: 1. That existing denominational colleges should bear a reasonable proportion to the denominational schools for which they were established; 2. That irresponsible and private managers who are uncontrolled in their admission or rejection of students, should not be allowed to monopolize the national work of training teachers; 3. That the best plan for supplementing the existing colleges would be the establishment and management of colleges under the control of local educational authorities subject to the supervision of the Education Department.

With regard to any shortcomings that may exist in the educational work done by the colleges, the "Minority" fully recognize the right of the training colleges to demand that the candidates for admission shall come to them with a more thorough education and a greater intellectual alertness, although they think that the colleges themselves need, not a more extensive curriculum, but a more thorough and intellectual study of the subjects in the curriculum, that the lecturers should be men who combine a wide knowledge of their subject with technical ability in handling classes, and that it would be well for the students in the colleges to come into contact with places of general education. *Efficiency of training colleges.*

The grants to the existing colleges is assented to, partly in deference to the strenuous desire of the advocates of denominational education to preserve a strongly denominational system of training with vigilant domestic discipline. It is not recommended that changes in the domestic arrangements which managers are unwilling to accept should be enforced upon them, but it is thought that so long as liberal opportunities of training are afforded no student should be expelled without his being entitled to appeal to the Education Department. The continuance of grants is acquiesced in in the hope that training will be associated with higher education, that greater facilities of training will be given to day students, and that the rights of conscience will be liberally recognized. The adoption of these reforms, it is anticipated, would lead to the employment of untrained teachers being dispensed with.* *Abolition of grants and domestic discipline.*

* On the points contained in this paragraph the "Minority" are unanimous in their opinion.

Day training colleges.

A large extension of facilities for training in day training colleges in connection with places of higher education existing, or to be established in various large towns throughout the country, is recommended, as well as the experimental establishment in one or two centres of a system of training somewhat on the lines indicated in the evidence of the Rev. E. F. M. MacCarthy. (See page 28.)

Third year of training.

The "Minority" also express an opinion that a third year of training would be of great value, and recommend that facilities should be given for this purpose to promising students, and that such students should be taught at some centre or centres in connection with places of higher education.

Government of new colleges.

As to the government of new training colleges, the opinion is expressed that it should be both of an educational and local representative character, and that perhaps a Council representative both of the higher education and of the School Boards in large towns (and in counties, where there are no large towns, a delegation of the county rating authority) might be constituted, working in conjunction with the Education Department.

CHAPTER VII.

RELIGIOUS INSTRUCTION.

Results of the Act of 1870.

REVIEWING the effects of the Act of 1870, and the restrictions thereby imposed on religious instruction given in elementary schools, the "Minority" come to the conclusion that those who believe in the great value of definite religious instruction in day schools, have no occasion to regard the results with dissatisfaction, and may congratulate themselves that, as compared with 1870, the number of children in denominational schools has enormously increased, and that the denominational instruction has been made more effective.

Probable effects of disturbing the settlement of 1870.

The further opinion is expressed that any attempt to disturb the settlement of 1870 by compelling all grant-aided schools to provide religious instruction would be a grave mistake from a denominational point of view, since any such attempt would be met with resolute resistance, which might end in diminishing rather than increasing the amount of religious teaching now given in elementary schools.

The contention of the Nonconformists, the "Minority" declare, is that in objecting to the provision of religious instruction in State-aided or rate-aided schools they do not maintain that the teachers under board or voluntary school managers are irreligious persons, but that it is impossible for board school managers, belonging to different churches, to take account of the religious qualifications in appointing teachers, and that, although it is required by the managers of denominational schools that teachers should be members of the churches with which the schools are connected, their general professional qualifications are likely to take precedence of their aptitude for giving religious instruction. *Contention of the Nonconformists.*

It is thought, however, to be unnecessary to discuss the present possibility or even the future desirability of Parliament determining that all schools should be secular. For the Nonconformists believe, the "Minority" go on to say, that the religious instruction of the children might safely be left to other agencies than the day school; but that, while they are all anxious that elementary schools receiving Parliamentary aid should be under the management of the representatives of the ratepayers, and should not form part of the equipment of churches, they are willing that the School Board of every district should determine for itself whether or not it shall make provision for religious teaching.*

In conclusion, attention is directed to the evidence of those witnesses who spoke as to the relations between public elementary schools and Sunday schools, and the extraordinary success which has attended Sunday schools in securing so large an attendance of scholars; " and," the " Minority " say, " whatever religious differences exist " with regard to the religious power of religious instruc" tion in day schools, there is none concerning the great " service which has been rendered by the religious instruc" tion given in Sunday schools to the moral and religious " life of the nation." *Sunday schools.*

---

* Mr. Heller records his strong conviction that the right of the teachers to give religious and moral instruction should not be interfered with, but that they should be at liberty at all times to support moral lessons by reference to religious sanctions.

CHAPTER VIII.

MORAL TRAINING.

Responsibility of managers and teachers.

IN the judgment of the "Minority," the moral instruction and training of the children are of paramount importance, but the responsibility rests on the managers and teachers, and unless they recognize its gravity the moral influence of schools will be ineffective.

Religious and moral training intimately connected.

It is recognized that for the great mass of the people of this country, religious and moral teaching are most intimately connected, and that in their judgment, the value and effectiveness of the latter depends to a very great extent upon religious sanctions. The "Minority" think that the present liberty of religious teaching, recognized by the law for local managers, is an ample security, and that so long as the present opinion of the country remains unchanged, the education of the children and the formation of their character will be based upon those principles which are dear to the mass of the people.*

Moral training.

With regard to moral training, the "Minority" say that it ought not to be assumed by managers that such training is satisfactory because an adequate time is devoted to religious teaching and observances; that religious teaching may be successful in giving to children a considerable knowledge of Christian doctrine and of the Bible, and even successful in creating a religious life, but yet may fail in developing and instructing the conscience. Great value is therefore attached to definite and systematic instruction in moral duties.

Depends on the quality of the teachers.

But the most admirable system of moral instruction, it is pointed out, will have no good effect unless the teachers themselves have high moral qualities, and the "Minority" say that in this respect they have exceptional pleasure in recalling the impression made upon them by most of the teachers who were examined by them.

As to the moral results.

The evidence of inspectors, teachers, and managers is referred to, who, on the whole, expressed their satisfaction with the moral results of the present educational system, and the "Minority" also are agreed in thinking that the moral teaching has been most valuable, and is largely

---

* On this paragraph the "Minority" are unanimous in their opinion.

owing to the personal influence of the teacher; further,
they say that it is not confined to specific religious teaching, but can also be given through secular illustrations.
Local interest, the influence of managers and parents, and
the personal character of the teacher, are looked to for
maintaining a high moral standard among the scholars;
the "Minority" also think it would be a misfortune if in
any way the duty of fully ascertaining the moral conduct
of a school were transferred from the inspector to the
managers.

CHAPTER IX.

CURRICULUM AND STAFF.

In considering the proper curriculum that may reasonably **Curriculum**
be required of an elementary school, it is recognized that **in infant**
a uniform curriculum cannot be expected of large town **schools.**
schools and small village schools. As regards infant
schools, the "Minority," whilst they are of opinion that
the principles laid down in Mr. Mundella's Code, and in
the instructions to inspectors, have had an excellent effect,
think that no pressure, direct or indirect, should be put
upon teachers to classify infants otherwise than according
to their attainments and intellectual and physical development. They agree that the infants should be so taught
in the infant school that on reaching the age of 8 or 9
they should be prepared to pass into, and receive the
instruction of, the senior department.

Satisfaction is expressed with the introduction into the
Code of simple object lessons as a necessary part of the
infant school teaching, and it is thought that still further
liberty might be conceded by literary instruction being
almost entirely dispensed with up to the age of 5, and in
some cases 6 years of age. The "Minority" think that
the work of the infant schools should be mainly formative,
and should guide the spontaneous activity of the child's
nature, and urge as of great importance that the teachers
for infant schools should be specially trained.

In small village schools with not more than 60 or 70 **Minimum**
in average attendance, the "Minority" agree with their **curriculum**

for infant schools. colleagues in their opinion of what should be the curriculum for scholars above the infant classes (see page 52).*

Staff in small rural schools. This course of instruction, it is thought, would probably necessitate more than one teacher; but where the head teacher is really competent, it is suggested that the services of monitors who are willing to stay on after the age of 13 for two or three years might be recognized in very small rural schools only.

The standards. The present sub-division of classes according to the existing standards is considered excessive for small schools, and it is thought that a division of the scholars, exclusive of the infants, into three classes, the work in each to represent a two years' course of study, would be more satisfactory in these schools.

Extra subjects. Where the managers are willing to strengthen the staff, and subject to the approval of the inspector, the "Minority" think that other subjects might be encouraged in the highest class of the school, especially if the parents are willing to permit longer hours of study for their children, in which case some further grant might be made, subject to the ordinary school work being thoroughly efficient.

Curriculum for medium schools. The "Minority" are of opinion that the same curriculum might be enforced more fully and thoroughly in schools with over 60 elder children in average attendance, and that where the children in a senior department exceed 100, a further and somewhat more detailed plan of studies might be laid down.

Curriculum for large schools. Where a department is large enough to employ two assistant teachers, so that the highest class has a teacher to itself, the "Minority" think that specific subjects might be taken up and taught with advantage, and that, although not insisted on, they should be encouraged.

Programmes of instruction suited to various classes of schools, it is recommended, should be drawn up by the Department, and that more detailed schemes of progressive teaching should be set forth in lieu of the present standards; freedom of choice too in following alternative courses being permitted to managers after consultation with the inspector.*

Higher elementary schools. The "Minority" recommend that, in any school district where the population within a radius of two miles amounts to 10,000, there should be a higher elementary school, or a higher department attached to an ordinary elementary school, with a curriculum suited to children

* On this point the "Minority" are unanimous in their opinion.

up to 14 or 15 years of age; that in more populous districts these schools should be increased; and that in districts where such departments cannot be established, children should be encouraged to continue their education beyond the ordinary school curriculum by the payment of grants, on the report of H.M. Inspector that the best arrangements have been made for their efficient instruction, due regard being paid to the difficulties and circumstances of each case.

The recommendation is made that in future a head teacher should count for 40 scholars instead of 60, a certificated assistant for 60 instead of 80, and an ex-pupil teacher for 50, a pupil-teacher in the third or fourth year for 30, and in the second year for 20; and that no others should be reckoned on the staff. Further it is recommended that pupil-teachers should be employed in pairs, so that the senior one mainly may be used to help in school work. *Strength of staff for ordinary schools.*

As it is thought that the services of persons of scholastic experience to inspect schools, to report on the teaching, and to help in remedying defects, would be of great value to managers, especially of voluntary schools, it is recommended that help should be given from the Government grant, not to exceed half the salary of such organizing teachers or inspectors, as may be appointed by a School Board or by a combination of Boards, or of voluntary managers, subject to the regulations of the Education Department. *Organizing masters.*

The "Minority" think the time has now come when certified efficient schools should no longer be included in the recognized school supply, unless they conform in every respect to the requirements imposed upon public elementary schools, and satisfy the inspector by an annual searching examination that they come up to the standard of a good school. *Certified efficient schools.*

With regard to Welsh schools the "Minority" agree with the recommendations of the "Majority" (see page 49), but it is pointed out that the peculiarities and difficulties of the Welsh-speaking population should be continually borne in mind in conducting the government examination and in any modifications of the regulations hereafter to be made by the central educational authority. *Welsh schools.*

For half-timers it is suggested that special modifications of the curriculum should be introduced either by spreading the progress of the scholars over a longer period, or by some simplification of the programme, and that the exist- *Half-time schools.*

ing difficulties will be met by educating them in separate departments, and by furnishing such schools with a specially strong staff.

Publication of the Code. Lastly, the "Minority" are of opinion that the Code should every year be published for the full time that it is required to be laid before Parliament, that no serious changes should be made without reasonable time being allowed for preparation, and that all extensions of the curriculum should be introduced gradually, and that great indulgence should be shown to schools taking them up for the first time for a year or two as to the higher stages.

Mr. Heller appends a note to the Report to the effect that he would recommend the abolition of the practice of endorsing teachers' parchment certificates, and that greater security should be given them in their tenure of office.

CHAPTER X.

TECHNICAL INSTRUCTION.

(ON THE CONCLUSIONS IN THIS CHAPTER THE "MINORITY" ARE UNANIMOUSLY AGREED.)

Definition. By technical instruction the "Minority" say they understand instruction in the principles and practice of domestic, commercial, agricultural, and industrial work.

Drawing. Of drawing, it is said that the recent graduated Syllabus of the Science and Art Department is likely to lead to its more satisfactory teaching and universal introduction in all boys' schools under trained teachers; and the evidence of witnesses who spoke as to drawing is regarded as practically unanimous in favour of its introduction into the elementary course. Regret is expressed that the examination is not at present conducted in such a way as to secure that due attention is paid to good methods of teaching drawing, and that no estimate is made by a competent examiner of the success and ability of the various teachers.

Workshop and science teaching. Some account is given in the Report of the instruction in the use of tools and science teaching conducted in certain schools in large towns, but the "Minority" having taken a general survey of the workshop instruction for boys in this country, find that very little is being done in this branch, as well as in drawing, and still less in that scientific education which is the foundation and most essential part of such technical instruction as can be given in the school.

The fact that, except in Sweden and France, no work- **Prolonged elementary instruction.** shop instruction is given in continental elementary schools, is said to indicate that the results of such instruction in this country ought to be carefully watched so that it does not thrust aside the older branches of technical instruction, especially drawing. Workshop instruction, it is thought, will be given most advantageously in the higher element- ary schools where scholars are trained first to make accurate drawings of the objects which they afterwards execute in the proper materials.

The true distinction between primary and secondary **Limits of primary and second- ary educa- tion.** instruction, the "Minority" think, is marked by the probable age at which the systematic instruction of the scholar is likely to cease, and that the curriculum for ordinary ele- mentary schools, for the majority of the scholars, should be one which can be completed on reaching the age of 14.

With regard to the introduction into the school curricu- **Manual instruction require- ments.** lum of instruction in methods which aim at developing handiness and accuracy, the following are enumerated as the requirements which it would be necessary to meet: suitable and roomy premises; a staff efficient, and one numerically sufficient; and inspectors with time enough to see and appreciate intelligent methods of teaching.

Assuming that these conditions are fulfilled, it is **Province of technical schools.** thought that technical schools with a course laid out for three years for scholars who have passed Standard VI might advantageously be founded in urban districts. These schools are not intended in any sense as places of apprenticeship for the pupils to the trades they in future wish to follow, but chiefly for the scientific and intellectual training of the scholars.

Such a system of technical schools, the "Minority" **Linked with elementary schools.** anticipate, would be the development and completion of the ordinary primary school course, and for scholars of a different class from those desiring secondary instruction. They suggest that the elder scholars, who need to develop their elementary education especially on the scientific side, should be grouped at a few centres, instead of being left in schools where they would be neglected for the duller and more backward children. The "Minority" agree with their colleagues as to the insufficient teaching of elementary scholars, which prevents them from taking advantage of higher technical education. (See page 56.)

Future Interpretation of "elementary technical education." The hope is expressed that, if the Technical Education Bill becomes law, the interpretation of the term "technical education" will be sufficiently wide to cover elementary commercial, agricultural, and industrial education. It is also pointed out that the Department must take security that a well-considered scheme of instruction, varying with the needs of the locality, shall be followed as a condition of Government aid.

CHAPTER XI.

EVENING CLASSES AND CONTINUATION SCHOOLS.

Continuation schools. THE "Minority" direct attention to the evanescent character of the knowledge acquired in the day school. This is attributed by them chiefly to the early age at which scholars leave school. It is considered necessary that those who pass Standard VI should be enabled to carry on their education in efficient continuation schools; and the "Minority" think that the systematizing of science and art classes, and the expansion of mechanics' institutes and other places of education, will supply the needs of this class of student.

Evening classes. Elementary evening classes are required, it is pointed out, not only for those who leave school without having obtained the full benefit of elementary education, but also for those who are more than 21 years of age.

Teachers in evening schools. It is thought that in towns and populous places young assistant teachers might undertake the duty of teachers in evening schools, and also trained teachers who have left the profession, although the aid of volunteers is chiefly relied on for this work.

Compulsory attendance. With regard to compulsory attendance at evening schools the opinion is expressed that attendance should be voluntary, though a limited amount of compulsion is suggested for those who have not reached Standard VI in the day school and are under 16 years of age.

In re-organizing the evening school system the follow-
ing points, it is recommended, should be kept in view:— Principles of evening school instruction.

1. That the need of young people for physical exercises
should be recognized.

2. That the methods and subjects of instruction should
be such as will awaken the interest of the pupils, and that
for this purpose the teaching should be mainly oral.

3. That the education, so far as it bears directly upon
the daily work of the scholars, both in its intellectual and
practical aspects, should be, if only in an elementary sense,
technical.

4. That the course of reading should be such as to fill
the minds and imaginations of the pupils with noble
examples of duty.

5. That music should be taught.

6. That it should be remembered that some pupils will
desire not so much the systematic continuation of their
education, as to supplement some special deficiency.

In conclusion the "Minority" express their opinion
that while the State should help evening schools as much
as possible, and that school boards should also direct their
local machinery towards the improvement and extension
of evening schools, yet that in this branch of education
every endeavour must be made to enlist voluntary activity
and co-operation.

CHAPTER XII.

GOVERNMENT INSPECTORS AND GOVERNMENT EXAMINATION.

The "Minority" are of opinion that in order to secure
efficiency, the annual examination of the work should be
searching, and that every child present on the day of
examination should be liable to be examined. Individual examination.

They are also of opinion that the examination, at least
up to and including the present Standard IV, should be
mainly oral, and framed with a view to ascertaining what
the children have been taught and how they have learnt
it, rather than an independent examination from the
inspector's standpoint. Oral examination.

I

Inspectors should be familiar with school work.

It is also thought that inspectors should be required to have familiarity not only with the elementary knowledge taught in schools, but also with the way in which it should be presented to the children.

Inspectors' report.

To guard against a negligent examination it is suggested that the inspector should draw up a report setting forth in detail the progress of the school, class by class, in the various subjects.

Inspection.

Great importance is attached to the work of inspection in ascertaining the value of the work, and the possibility of improving it, and the " Minority " are of opinion that in order to do it well, the inspector must thoroughly understand school keeping, and must either have been a successful teacher – not necessarily in elementary schools—or have been long familiar with schools ; that he must also have a pleasant manner and sympathy with children, tact and judgment in dealing with school boards and managers, and be a man of wide and liberal education and cultivation.

They are further of opinion that the inspectorate should be open throughout to elementary teachers, which might induce men of wide education to become teachers in elementary schools.

Inspectors' assistants.

The commencing salaries of inspectors' assistants are thought to be too low, and it is recommended that they should be raised to £200 a year, and that the limits of age should range from 25 to 40.

Visits without notice.

Much value is attached to visits without notice, and the "Minority" wish to see them more frequent, so as to enable inspectors to judge better of the efficiency of the pupil-teachers and probationers.

Uniformity of standard.

In order to secure uniformity of standard it is suggested that the quality of education to be given to the children should be, as far as possible, uniform, and that a lower standard should not be required in the country than in the town, nor in small schools than in large schools. The inability of country children to learn as easily as town children is considered to be often exaggerated, and results from the necessary smallness of the schools, and low salaries of the teachers, the more capable in consequence seeking town appointments. The local conferences now held among inspectors are regarded as a valuable feature, but it is recommended that educational conferences should be held under the guidance of the inspector, where managers, school officers, and teachers might discuss educational questions. Lastly, the " Minority " think that it would be a good thing if the chief inspector had no special district

of his own, or that it should be so small that his time
should be expended in inspecting all the districts under
his supervision.

CHAPTER XIII.

THE PARLIAMENTARY GRANT.

(ON THE CONCLUSIONS IN THIS CHAPTER THE "MINORITY" ARE UNANIMOUSLY AGREED.)

THE present method of distributing the Parliamentary **Payment**
grant, the "Minority" say, has been criticised with more **by results.**
energy than almost any other part of the educational
system, especially that part of it which makes the payment follow closely the percentage of success calculated
on individual passes. Having fully summarised the evidence on this question, the "Minority" are of opinion that
the amount of the grant paid must vary to some extent
with the ascertained efficiency of the school as tested
by the Government inspection, at any rate, whilst popular
education continues so largely under voluntary management.

With regard to the future payment of the Parliamentary **Conclu-**
grant, the following conclusions are arrived at:— **sions.**

1. That the most satisfactory way of securing
efficiency in elementary schools, and of escaping the
injurious results of the present system, would be the
organization of our national education under representative management over areas of sufficient extent, subject
to State inspection, which should rather aim at securing
that the local authorities do their duty, than at testing
minutely the results of instruction.

2. That the present method of assessing payment on
the standard subjects should be discontinued.

3. That a large portion of the grant should be fixed,
subject to the condition that better guarantees of
efficiency are secured, both as regards buildings, teachers,
and curriculum.

4. That more money should be paid to provide grants
for teaching such subjects as cookery, science, and drawing,
and for providing organizing masters, and means of instructing the pupil-teachers.

5. That the remainder of the capitation grant which is variable, should be apportioned among the various subjects of instruction, and that the inspector should look rather to the quality of the work than to the percentage of scholars who show some knowledge.

6. That where a fuller curriculum for a school seems reasonable, more aid should be given to meet the corresponding efforts of managers.

7. That special aid should be given to small village schools.

8. That the capitation grant should increase with the lowness of the fee, and diminish with the raising of the fee above the average of the country.

An amendment representing the views of Dr. Dale and Mr. Heller, moved on a passage in the chapter on this subject in the Report of the Commission, is here appended, and gives their reasons for wishing to abandon altogether the system of "payment by results."

CHAPTER XIV.

COMPULSION.

(ON THE CONCLUSIONS CONTAINED IN THIS CHAPTER THE "MINORITY" ARE UNANIMOUSLY AGREED.)

Effect of present system. AFTER tracing the history and growth of legislation for compulsory school attendance, the "Minority" express their opinion that, although, in some districts, there may be a disposition to remove children prematurely from school in order to put them to work, this is due to the low legal minimum of compulsion, and not to any dislike to the system. But, taking the country throughout, they think that the effect of the introduction of legal compulsion has not been merely a great increase in the number of children under instruction, but a considerable prolongation of school life.

Local authorities. As to the ineffectiveness of the present system urged by many witnesses, the laxity of School Attendance Committees and small rural School Boards is admitted, although it is thought that they are discouraged by the action of the magistrates.

The "Minority" express the hope that magistrates and others will operate more heartily in enforcing the law, and they look to the growth of public opinion in its favour, rather than to increased legal penalties for securing regular attendance. Further, they consider that the bulk of improvement in attendance is due to the better school provision. and improvement in the instruction and the curriculum; the further growth in numbers, regularity, and punctuality, being looked to for increased improvement in schools.

It is thought that the time has now come when the law should be strengthened, that magistrates should be required to give effect to it, and that repeated offences within a certain time should entail a heavier penalty.

The recommendation is made that, where a child is said to be under instruction in a school not recognized as efficient, it should be lawful for the school authority to require such a child to present himself for examination at a public elementary school near where he lives, and failing to satisfy H.M. Inspector, the certificate of the Inspector should be evidence that he is not efficiently instructed. *Children not attending certified efficient schools.*

It is thought that the substitution of distress warrants for the power of committal is cumbrous and costly, and has injuriously affected the working of the law of compulsory attendance. *Distress warrants.*

With regard to industrial schools, the "Minority" think that their educational work should be under the inspection of the Education Department. Truant schools, with a short period of initial detention, but with power to take the boy back, should be substituted, it is suggested, in many cases for the ordinary industrial school, long detention at which is regarded as not applicable to those cases where a short period of sharp discipline would be more suitable. *Industrial and Truant Schools.*

It is recommended that the ordinary minimum age of exemption from school attendance should be 11 for half-timers, subject to their having attained the Third Standard, to be raised in two or three years to the Fourth; and that, except in very special circumstances to be considered by the local authority, 13 should be the age for total exemption, but that children not profitably employed at work should be obliged to attend school till the age of 14. *Age of exemption.*

CHAPTER XV.

SCHOOL MANAGEMENT.

COMPARISON OF BOARD AND VOLUNTARY SCHOOLS.

Denominational management. WITH reference to the denominational question, the "Minority" do not consider the conscience clause an adequate security for fair play and religious impartiality in the management, but recognize that it must continue so long as the country delegates the duty of public education to volunteers mainly influenced by denominational zeal.

Inspectors' reports. A strong opinion is expressed that the inspectors' reports on schools should be fully made known throughout the districts, which would not only prove useful information to parents, but would also in the case of weak schools exercise useful pressure on managers.

School accounts. The "Minority" are also of opinion that the accounts of all schools receiving public money should be audited with equal thoroughness, and that the same rules of legality should be applied to their expenditure.

Fees. With regard to the fees it is observed that they should be fair and uniform, should include all school charges, and should be approved by the Department for voluntary schools as in the case of board schools.

"Farmed" schools. The "farming" of schools is regarded as very objectionable, and the same evils are said to be likely to exist in small schools where the teacher's salary is dependent on the fees and grant; the evils, amongst others, likely to arise are said to be over-pressure, cramming, and undue reduction of staff.

In conclusion it is thought that nothing short of public responsible management by representative bodies drawn from a sufficiently large district will completely remove existing dangers.[*]

Comparison between board and voluntary schools. Taking the government inspection as a fair test, the efficiency of board schools is regarded by the "Minority" as undoubtedly superior to that of voluntary schools.

They agree with the contention that this is because Boards are not hampered by want of money, and because large schools are better than small ones, advantages which

---

[*] On the conclusions in these paragraphs the "Minority" are unanimously agreed.

board schools as a rule enjoy, and which are regarded as arguments in favour of the extension of the system of board schools.

But apart from this another reason for the alleged superior efficiency of board schools is said to be that having several schools to manage, Boards are thereby educated in their work; and the opinion is expressed that the areas of School Boards should be so extended that no board should exist with only one or two schools under it. Again it is said that in many voluntary schools the management often falls officially into the hands of unfit persons whom there is no power to remove, while Boards can rectify such an error in three years. *Reasons for the alleged superior efficiency of board schools.*

The "Minority" are agreed in thinking that owing to the poverty of voluntary schools, inspectors have lowered their standard even below the Code minimum for fear of shutting up schools which depend upon the grant for existence, and yet fall below the standard of teaching which would deserve recognition and payment; a danger, they say, against which it is most important to guard. *Conclusion.*

The results of the statistical inquiries made by the Commission and other evidence are examined and reviewed at some length in the Report, for the purpose of showing the superiority of board schools over voluntary schools, and the chapter concludes with the following expression of opinion : " We think that we are justified in concluding that School Board management, by securing a sufficient area of collective supervision, by its command of sufficient funds for the due maintenance of schools, by its greater facilities for building schools large enough to secure efficient organization, is better able to promote national education than the voluntary system ; that already the results of board school teaching are proved to be distinctly superior to the education provided in voluntary schools ; that there is evidence to show that the standard of educational efficiency is kept down out of tenderness to the want of means of voluntary schools, and that a lower standard is applied to them, avowedly in the matter of school buildings and furniture, and also to some extent in the estimating of the results of examination."

CHAPTER XVI.

COST OF PUBLIC ELEMENTARY EDUCATION.

School fees and free education. WITH regard to the demand that school fees should be abolished, the "Minority" are not agreed in principle on the question whether fees should form a part of the sources of income for a compulsory system of national education. To the question, should the loss which would result from the abolition of school fees be made good from local or national sources? the answer given by the "Minority" is that they are compelled in the interest of education to conclude that no practical scheme of free education compatible with the continuance of the voluntary system has presented itself to them.*

Grievances of the present fee system. It is said that substantial grievances exist in connection with the fee question, and in order to reduce its practical hardships to the poor to a minimum, and to prevent the imposition of varying fees in the same school from being used as a means of oppression and of selection and exclusion of scholars, many corrections are needed. The opinion is expressed: (i.) That it is the duty of the Department to secure that the fee shall not be beyond the means of the parents, but that if a School Board proposes a low fee, they are the elected representatives of the ratepayers on whom the loss will fall, and that the Department should not interfere for the purpose of raising the fee; (ii.) That in no case should the fee be raised with the standard in which the child is working; (iii.) That it should cover all school charges, and that where the school is the only one, or the other schools with lower fees are full, it should have a prescribed maximum of a moderate amount.

Fees paid by guardians. As to the payment of fees by guardians, the following recommendations are made: That it should be the duty

---

* On this point the "Minority" are unanimous in their opinion, with the exception of Mr. Buxton, who regards the evidence on the whole in favour of a permissive system of free schools. He suggests that the managers of any public elementary school, if they desire to abolish the fees, should be entitled to demand an additional grant from the Consolidated Fund, to be calculated on the general average of the fees throughout the country, and on the average attendance at the school in question.

of the guardians to pay the fees of all children, whether under five or past the standard for exemption, whose parents wish to send them to school, and who are otherwise fit for exemption; that in the case of out-door paupers the guardians should pay all fees direct to the managers, and not give a lump sum to the parents to include fees; and that if the guardians retain the duty of paying fees, they should entertain applications at places convenient to the applicants and away from the workhouse, and that they should make arrangements, especially in rural districts, in the different villages for hearing applications.

Since at present it is the town schools with high fees *Special aid to schools with low fees.* which receive very high grants, and the struggling village schools, or those amongst the poorest in large towns with low fees, which earn low grants, the "Minority" suggest that in all schools, if the fee income for the year is between 9s. and 10s. per child in average attendance, the fixed grant should be augmented by 6d. a head, and increased 6d. for each 1s. diminution of fee income; and that schools receiving from 11s. to 12s. a head from fees should be subject to a diminution of 6d. on the fixed grant, diminishing 6d. for each increase of 1s. on fee income up to £1 a head from fees.

Further, it is recommended that School Boards should have full power if they see fit to make some or all of their schools free.

In connection with this question the case of poor children who need food as well as education is considered, and the hope is expressed that managers will provide, where necessary, a system of self-supporting dinners, though no recommendation is made as to free dinners.

With the contention urged by many witnesses that the *The Government grant, 17s. 6d. limit.* 17s. 6d. limit should be relaxed or repealed, the "Minority" do not agree, and say, "at any rate, we are entitled to expect a substantial amount of local contribution before the State gives more than 17s. 6d."

In considering the proposal to give aid from local rates *Aid to voluntary schools from rates.* to denominational schools, the "Minority" say that it seems to them impracticable and politically inexpedient, first on account of the religious difficulty of directly subsidising schools where different theological dogmas are taught, and where the teachers are limited to distinct denominations; and secondly, on account of the greater difficulty of giving aid without local control. It is pointed out that such aid must be either optional or compulsory; if the former, the old church rate controversy would be revived in every district; and if the latter, it would be necessary to give the local contributors a share of the management. They therefore do not see their way to support a proposal to impose on the ratepayers a contribution in support of voluntary elementary schools.*

Lord Lingen's and Mr. Cumin's schemes. As to Lord Lingen's and Mr. Cumin's schemes in favour of decentralising the administration and support of elementary education, and more closely connecting the ratepayers with their representatives and the denominational schools, the "Minority" are of opinion that such large changes would not be acceptable to the mass of voluntary managers, who value highly their present direct relations with the Education Department, and that the consideration of so extensive a revolution must be consequent on any new scheme of local self-government that may pass into law.

Aid for small village schools. For small village schools further aid is thought to be necessary, and it is recommended that, where there is an isolated school with no other school nearer than two miles, and with an average attendance below 100, a grant should be paid, increasing by 6s. 8d. for each child by which the attendance falls below 100 up to a maximum grant of £20; subject to the conditions that a certificated head teacher of experience and efficiency is employed at a minimum salary of £60, and the requirement by the Department of a proper curriculum.

CHAPTER XVII.

LOCAL ELEMENTARY SCHOOL AUTHORITIES.

Relative positions of board and voluntary schools. As to what should be the relative positions of School Boards and voluntary school managers, the evidence of the advocates of the voluntary system is in the direction that much advantage results to education from the rivalry of the two systems, and the "Minority" are disposed to admit that such is the case to this extent, that the denominational

---

* On this point the "Minority" are unanimous in their opinion.

system is forced to justify its existence by redoubled exertions when brought into contact with the School Board system.

They are also of opinion that, having regard to the large share now taken in national education by voluntary bodies, it would not be a practical proposal to transfer the whole maintenance and management of elementary schools to public representative bodies. But they state their conviction that the districts where no School Boards exist, and where there is consequently no educational competition, have suffered severely not only in educational efficiency, but from unsatisfactory buildings and furniture, absence of playgrounds, a narrowed curriculum, and high fees. The Nonconformists also, it is said, have to submit to a school permeated by the influence of an unsympathetic, and often hostile, church organization, in the management of which they have no voice, and it is hoped that amongst the changes imminent in local government, provision will be made to remedy this state of things.* *Effect on districts where no School Boards exist.*

The special Noncomformist grievance is dealt with more fully in a separate chapter of this Report, but as regards the political objection to confiding the mass of national education to private managers with special denominational interests, the "Minority" say that even though the present system is too widely established to be superseded, yet in future the policy of the country should be directed towards the extension of a popular and comprehensive system, rather than of one privately managed and based on sectarian differences. *As to the future organization of national education.*

They recommend, therefore, that the smaller rural School Boards should be united, and, provided that the areas of administration are sufficiently large, and no School Board exists, that there should be a local representative authority to supply and manage new schools;* and that the local element should be considered in any scheme of representation. *Recommendations.*

It is also recommended that, where there is a reasonable number of persons desiring them, there should be schools of an undenominational character, and under popular representative government.*

The present method of electing School Boards by the cumulative vote is regarded as unsatisfactory, and the "Minority" are not favourable to any form of proportional *Election of School Boards.*

* On this point the "Minority" are unanimous in their opinion.

representation. The opinion is expressed that the larger towns should be divided into wards, returning, if any form of proportional representation be retained, not more than five members each, and that for this purpose the single transferable vote is preferable to the present cumulative vote (see p. 89).

It is thought premature to consider the question whether School Boards might be superseded by new local representative bodies until the new local authorities have been constituted, and a considerable experience of their working has been gained.

CHAPTER XVIII.

COMPLAINTS OF THE ADVOCATES OF DENOMINATIONAL SCHOOLS.

School supply.

THE first complaint made by the supporters of denominational schools noticed by the "Minority" is that owing to the prior right of School Boards to supply needed accommodation, church organizations may be prevented from building schools suited to the wants of their supporters, or may at any rate be excluded from sharing in the annual grant. In reference to the interpretation of the word "suitable" as used in Section V of the Act of 1870 (see note, page 1), the "Minority" say that no doubt the law only imposes the obligation of building schools in the case of a School Board, but that it would seem equitable where (in the ordinary acceptation of the word) the people for whom the schools exist show that they do not consider them "suitable," by frequenting others, that the State should not exclude these schools, if efficient, from the annual grants.* It is pointed out that the same principle would apply where School Boards desire to build on account of the popularity of their schools and the great pressure upon them. It is regarded as a fair concession to minorities that liberty should be given to them to establish distinctive and denominational schools under private, and largely under clerical management, where the general

Interpretation of the word "suitable."

---

* On this point the "Minority" are unanimous in their opinion.

school system is popular and representative; but the circumstances are materially altered, the Report goes on to say, if this liberty to found exclusive schools prevents the mass of the people from having the control of the management and the appointment of the teachers in the schools to which they are by law forced to send their children.

Another ground of complaint is that School Boards have built excessively, and thereby closed efficient voluntary schools. Three cases are examined in the Report where this was alleged to be the case, namely, at Sheffield, Hull, and at the Upper Kennington Lane Board School, London, and the conclusion of the "Minority" is that if the facts are examined broadly, the growth of the board school system will be found to have been accompanied by a great improvement and expansion of the voluntary schools. *Alleged undue multiplication of board schools.*

The "Minority" assert that the pledge given in 1870 that the board system was to supplement and not to supplant the voluntary system, has been kept, and more than kept, as shown by the fact that by the help of that Act the grant to voluntary schools has increased, and the subscriptions have diminished. *The pledge of 1870 has been kept.*

A further complaint by voluntary subscribers is that they have to pay rates for the support of board schools which they dislike, besides subscribing to their own schools. This complaint the "Minority" think unreasonable. *Complaint that voluntary subscribers have to pay rates.*

The proposal made by some that they should be excused from payment of the school rate to the extent to which they subscribe to their own schools is not regarded by the "Minority" as practical, even if it were theoretically reasonable. It is pointed out that since voluntary schools are supported not in obedience to a legal obligation, but because their subscribers wish to maintain distinct denominational teaching, as well as the control and management of the schools, it is not unreasonable that for these important powers and other incidental advantages which are secured, they should bear some material part of the cost of preserving them.

For the complaint as to the rating of school buildings, the "Minority" are of opinion that as no profit can legally be made by elementary school managers, it would be equitable that public elementary schools in premises conveyed by a trust deed free for the purposes of education should be exempt from rating. *Rating of school buildings.*

As to remission of fees.

Another grievance urged by the advocates of voluntary schools is that whereas school boards very generally use their power to remit fees, voluntary managers cannot easily afford to sacrifice that source of income, and have to send the poor to the guardians to obtain payment.

The "Minority" repeat their recommendation that the poor are fairly entitled to free schooling, and that, if necessary, a moderate fee ought to be paid for them by some public authority. To remove any idea of pauperism, it is suggested that the new district councils might perhaps be entrusted with this duty.

As to the competition of board schools.

With reference to the complaint that voluntary managers are too poor to permit them to keep up to the standard of the board schools, the "Minority" say that it is unreasonable to object to the progress of education on account of limited means; that voluntary management implies voluntary effort, and that if the effort is inadequate there is no duty imposed on them to maintain their schools, which are now a much lighter burden than they were ten years ago.

CHAPTER XIX.

THE GRIEVANCES OF NONCONFORMISTS.

The Act of 1870.

THE theory of the Act of 1870, the "Minority" say, is that the grant is given for the secular instruction only, and they proceed to inquire whether the provisions of that Act for securing the rights of parents are effective. Having fully summarised the evidence with regard to the conscience clause, the conclusion is arrived at that though rarely violated, it is wholly ineffective, and that the protection it is supposed to offer to parents whose children are attending schools where the religious instruction is contrary to their own religious belief, is illusory.

The conscience clause is ineffective.

Reasons why children are not withdrawn.

The following reasons are given for the non-withdrawal of children from religious instruction :—

1. That to large numbers of parents the existence of the right to withdraw their children is unknown.

2. That some parents are unwilling to appeal to it through fear of the disfavour of managers and teachers towards their children.

3. That in the rural districts Nonconformists apprehend that if they withdraw their children, they and their children may suffer annoyance and loss at the hands of the clergy and adherents of the Church of England.

4. That some parents feel that, since the clergyman and his friends contribute to the support of the school in which their children are educated, there would be something dishonourable in withdrawing their children from the religious instruction for which the school is maintained.

Further, it is said, that those districts where the schools connected with the Church of England are the only ones accessible to the population, the entrance into the teaching profession is practically closed against Nonconformists. To meet this grievance it is thought that the following proposal accepted at the Wesleyan Methodist Conference of 1873, might be adopted; viz., that in justice to the interests of national education in the broadest sense, and to the different religious denominations of the country, School Boards should be established everywhere, and an undenominational school placed within reasonable distance of every family. *Exclusion of Nonconformists from the teaching profession.*

The chapter closes with the following recommendations:— *Recommendations.*

1. That every parent shall be provided with a printed statement, drawn up by the Department, informing him of his right to withdraw his child from the religious instruction, and that the child will thereby be subjected to no disadvantage.

2. That in schools where there is a class-room and more than one teacher, secular instruction shall be given in a separate room during the hour of religious instruction to such children as are withdrawn.*

3. That where there is no class-room and only one teacher, children withdrawn from religious teaching shall not be required to attend till the time for secular instruction begins, and shall be dismissed when it is over.*

4. That no child shall be charged a higher fee either for not attending the Sunday School in connection with the day school, or because he is withdrawn from the religious instruction given in the day school.

To this chapter a note is appended by Mr. Lyulph Stanley and Mr. Heller, to the effect that while they accept these expressions of grievances as accurate and concur in the recommendations, they are of opinion that the small

* On this point the " Minority " are unanimous in their opinion.

.